Angels

Angels

A History

DAVID ALBERT JONES

OXFORD
UNIVERSITY PRESS

Angels

A History

DAVID ALBERT JONES

OXFORD
UNIVERSITY PRESS

OXFORD
UNIVERSITY PRESS

Great Clarendon Street, Oxford OX2 6DP

Oxford University Press is a department of the University of Oxford.
It furthers the University's objective of excellence in research, scholarship,
and education by publishing worldwide in

Oxford New York

Auckland Cape Town Dar es Salaam Hong Kong Karachi
Kuala Lumpur Madrid Melbourne Mexico City Nairobi
New Delhi Shanghai Taipei Toronto

With offices in

Argentina Austria Brazil Chile Czech Republic France Greece
Guatemala Hungary Italy Japan Poland Portugal Singapore
South Korea Switzerland Thailand Turkey Ukraine Vietnam

Oxford is a registered trade mark of Oxford University Press
in the UK and in certain other countries

Published in the United States
by Oxford University Press Inc., New York

British Library Cataloguing in Publication Data

Data available

Library of Congress Cataloging in Publication Data

Library of Congress Control Number: 2009941588

Typeset by SPI Publisher Services, Pondicherry, India
Printed in the UK by
MPG Books Group Ltd

ISBN 978-0-19-958295-2

3 5 7 9 10 8 6 4 2

To Eustace, that she and I may find mercy
and that we may grow old together.

(Tobit 8: 7)

CONTENTS

PICTURE ACKNOWLEDGEMENTS

Picture Acknowledgements

PREFACE

Angels. We all know what they look like. They have wings and halos. They appear in children's nativity plays. They wear long white robes, apart from cherubs, who are like naked fat little children. They live in heaven on clouds but come to earth to guard or to guide. They are portrayed in stained-glass windows and look down protectively from gravestones, but they also appear in films, cartoons, and even adverts, encouraging us to do the right thing while little devils tempt us to do the wrong thing. The ones on the Christmas tree look female, but in films they are often played by men (John Travolta, Nicholas Cage, Denzel Washington, and Cary Grant have all played angels).

Angels are acknowledged in each of the three great 'Abrahamic' religions—Judaism, Christianity, and Islam—and among Christians their appeal is broad enough to extend from Russian Orthodoxy to American Evangelical Protestantism. Those post-Christian forms of spirituality, which are sometimes termed 'New Age', also lay claim to the guidance and healing of angels. While church attendance, at least in Western Europe, has declined, angels are as popular as ever. In an age that prides itself on scientific rationality, belief

Figure 1 Children dress up as angels for a nativity play.

in angels seems not quite respectable. Yet these ethereal beings are now the subject of innumerable references, depictions, and allusions in the electronic ether. At the time of writing, an Internet search for 'angel' registered 287,000,000 hits, which was, for example, five times as many as 'Christianity' and six times as many as 'astronomy'.

What, then, is an angel? And where do our ideas and images of angels come from? This book outlines some of the more prominent stories and speculations about angels in Judaism, Christianity, and Islam, and in contemporary culture. It reflects on the way that angels have been portrayed in art, literature, and cinema. Nevertheless, this book is not only a history but also an examination of some of the implications of angels: why people find the idea of angels attractive, helpful, or consoling; why they remain so powerful in modern culture; and thus what angels may tell us about ourselves.

The first chapter provides a chronology of how the understanding of angels developed in Judaism and then in Christianity and Islam. The second chapter is a chronological overview of the representation of angels. It also addresses two particular questions in regard to images of angels: the portrayal of 'cherubs' and the portrayal of the gender of angels. These two chapters set out a mental map and a chronology of angels within religions and in the wider culture. They establish points of reference for the rest of the book.

The third chapter considers what kind of being an angel would be. It introduces Thomas Aquinas's treatise on the angels. Thomas's treatise remains perhaps the most sophisticated attempt to give an account of what a purely spiritual creature would be like.

The next four chapters are thematic and consider some characteristic features of angels: angels as messengers; angels as guardians; angels in heaven; and angels that have fallen. In each case the discussion draws on the resources of the three Abrahamic religions as well as art, literature, philosophy, and human experience.

The final chapter argues that these stories and speculations about angels can help to illuminate aspects of human existence. The meaning of angels in religion and in popular culture has varied, but they have often been carriers of a counter-cultural message. Angels sometimes wrestle against us. They help unmask our prejudices, among which is the unfounded prejudice that human beings are alone in an empty universe.

Reflecting on the implications of angels in relation to contemporary culture can help retrieve a sense of human beings, not as masters of a world that is devoid of meaning, but as pilgrims sensitive to moments when meaning is revealed.

This whole book is about angels, but for the most part it seeks neither to prove nor to disprove the existence of angels, neither to assert nor to debunk. Ancient texts are therefore approached from a narrative perspective, asking what the story says or implies, and how it has been read by later readers. This is not to deny that texts have a history and often a prehistory. Stories may emerge from experience or imagination or both. They are told and retold. They are written in one context and may be revised and edited for another context. Nevertheless, once the form of the story is fixed we can ask what the story says. What is it about? What does it say about these creatures called angels? It is difficult to avoid entirely the question of the existence of angels, and occasionally the author's own view will show through. The last chapter will explicitly address the question of whether we can and should keep an open mind about the existence of angels. Nevertheless, in the main this book seeks not to judge one way or another. Rather it explores how people have sought to make sense of their belief in angels. I hope that the result is a book that is informative and entertaining for believer and sceptic alike.

1

A Brief History of Angels

Angels and Abraham

And the Lord appeared to him by the oaks of Mamre, as he sat at the door of his tent in the heat of the day. He lifted up his eyes and looked, and behold, three men stood in front of him. When he saw them, he ran from the tent door to meet them, and bowed himself to the earth, and said, 'My lord, if I have found favour in your sight, do not pass by your servant. Let a little water be brought, and wash your feet, and rest yourselves under the tree, while I fetch a morsel of bread, that you may refresh yourselves, and after that you may pass on—since you have come to your servant.'   (Genesis 18: 1–5)

Who are these three figures who emerge from the shimmering heat to visit the old man resting in the shade of an ancient oak? They are angels, and the old man is Abraham. This is one of the first mentions of angels in one of the earliest parts of the Hebrew Scriptures. In its present written form this passage is perhaps around three thousand years old, but the story itself is certainly older, part of a cycle of stories about Abraham, Isaac, and Jacob, which would have been passed on orally, part of the story of the Jewish people.

Figure 2 For Andrei Rublev the hospitality of Abraham was also an image of the Holy Trinity.

The New Testament alludes to the encounter of Abraham and the angels (Hebrews 13: 2) and the theme was popular among early Christian writers. In the Middle Ages the greatest Russian iconographer, Andrei Rublev (c.1360–1430), made this story the subject of his most famous icon: *The Hospitality of Abraham* or *The Holy Trinity*. Rublev, as a Christian, interpreted the three angels as representing God, who is three-in-one: Father, Son, and Holy Spirit.

The same encounter is related in the Quran (51: 24–8), where the angels say, 'Peace', and Abraham replies, 'Peace to you, strangers!' In the Hebrew account Abraham stands near the strangers as they are eating. However, in the Quran, the strangers do not eat, and it is precisely at this point that Abraham starts to become aware that they are angels. For in Islamic tradition angels do not eat.

The story of the hospitality of Abraham belongs to the oldest strand of religious tradition to speak about angels. It is a story that is common to Jews, Christians, and Muslims. As will become clear below, there are subsequent developments in the way that angels are described in the Hebrew Scriptures and in later Judaism. There are also further developments within the Christian tradition. At some points there are differences between Christianity and Islam on angels, as, for example, on the question of whether the Devil is a fallen angel. Nevertheless, what is most immediately striking is that angels are companions of Abraham; they occur in the stories of Abraham in the earliest forms we have. It is also noteworthy that the religions that claim Abraham as their father, Judaism, Christianity, and Islam, all continue to tell stories of angels. Jesus, in one of his parables, speaks of the poor man who dies and is 'carried by the angels to Abraham's bosom' (Luke 16: 22). There is, then, an enduring connection between Abraham and the angels.

Angels before the Exile

The angels who visit Abraham are described as three men (Genesis 18: 2). There is clearly something that sets them apart, as Abraham recognizes that 'the Lord' is visiting him, but they are still described as 'men'. These angels have no wings or halos, and they are not named.

At this stage in Hebrew thought, as evident in the books of Genesis, Numbers, Judges, and Joshua, angels do not show a great deal of personality. They deliver the message that is given them to deliver, and do what they are sent to do, but they do not have names of their own or stories of their own to distinguish them from other angels. A partial exception is the stranger whom Joshua meets with a sword in his hand. Joshua asks him, 'Are you one of us or one of our adversaries?' He replies, 'Neither, but I have come as commander of the army of the Lord' (Joshua 5: 13–15). It seems that here is an angel with a particular role, but still the angel has no name.

The book of Judges repeats the refrain 'in those days, there was no king in Israel' (Judges 18: 1, 19: 1, 21: 25). Military leaders or 'judges' assumed command when the need arose, to fight against an external enemy, but there was no stable unified hierarchy. It was around 1000 BCE that Saul established a united kingdom over Israel, with David later establishing Jerusalem as its capital. It seems that it was at this point that the people started to refer to God as 'the Lord of hosts'. This title is especially popular in the books of 1 and 2 Samuel, 1 and 2 Kings, Isaiah, and Jeremiah. God is here imagined as a king surrounded by his heavenly armies, his 'hosts'. For example, the prophet Micaiah says to the king of Israel, 'I saw the Lord sitting on his throne, and all the host of heaven standing beside him on his right hand and on his left' (1 Kings 22: 19). God sits on a throne with a heavenly army and the soldiers in this army are angels.

From the time that Israel became a kingdom, the angels of God were imagined as a heavenly army, but there was not at first any clear idea of different ranks of angels. However, there was already in the earliest tradition reference to one very distinct kind of angelic being: the cherubim. These are given the task of guarding paradise to prevent the first human beings from returning there (Genesis 3: 24). They are also mentioned as carved figures on the 'ark of the covenant'—the box that Moses makes to house the Ten Commandments (Exodus 25: 18). Later, in the book of Isaiah, reference is made to another distinct kind of angel, the six-winged seraphim (Isaiah 6: 2).

Angels after the Exile

In 586 BCE the King of Judah was defeated in battle and Jerusalem was captured by the Babylonians. Many of the people were taken into exile in Babylon (in modern Iraq). This had a great effect on their religious beliefs, including their beliefs about angels. This was recognized by the Jews themselves. According to later Jewish tradition, 'the names of the angels were brought by the Jews from Babylon'.

The book of Job was written after the Jews had returned from exile. It is one of the 'wisdom writings', not a book of laws or prophecies, and not a book on the history of Israel. Wisdom books contain general reflections on the human condition. In the case of Job, the focus is the suffering of an innocent man. In relation to angels, this book is important for introducing the figure of the Satan (in Hebrew), also called the Devil (in Greek), the accuser who tempts Job to curse God.

The book of Daniel is set during the period of exile in Babylon, but most scholars think that the book was written much later, in the period of the Maccabean revolt (around 165 BCE). The book of Daniel marks an important stage in the development of ideas about angels. It has a concept of different ranks of angels and of angels appointed to watch over different cities and nations. This book gives the names of two angels: Michael and Gabriel.

The book of Daniel was the last book of the undisputed Hebrew Scriptures to be written. Among other Jewish religious books written around the same time is the book of Tobit. This book was widely admired as a moral tale, and over the centuries it has been a popular subject for artists. It tells the story of how God sends an angel, Raphael, to heal Tobit. Raphael is described as 'one of the seven angels who see the face of God' (Tobit 12: 15), but the names of the other six angels are not given.

It is another Jewish book, the book of Enoch, that first gives the names of seven 'archangels'—Uriel, Raphael, Raguel, Michael, Saraqael, Gabriel, and Remiel—as well as naming various other angels, including Jeremiel. Enoch also tells the story of the fall of angels and is quoted in the New Testament (Jude 14–15). A little later, another Jewish book, 2 Esdras, also mentions Uriel and Jeremial. This book was popular among early Christian writers and was included in an appendix to Romans Catholic Bibles. It is quoted in the traditional Catholic prayers for the dead.

While Daniel, Tobit, and Enoch were being written, Jewish scholars were translating the Hebrew Scriptures into Greek. The earliest and most influential translation is called the Septuagint (abbreviated LXX), because of a story that it was the work of seventy men, each of whom independently produced an identical translation! The story has no basis in history, but it is a good story, and the name stuck. The Septuagint translation was produced at a time when the Jews were becoming more interested in angels, and so it tends to add in references to angels that are not explicit in the original. For example, the Septuagint translation of Deuteronomy 32: 8 states that God 'established the bounds of the nations according to the number of the angels of God'. The Hebrew text of this passage does not refer to 'the angels of God'.

The period after the return from exile saw a shift in Jewish views on angels: there was a greater concern with hierarchies, ranks, or numbers of angels; there was a growing devotion to a particular guardian angel assigned to each person; there was increasing talk about demons and the figure of a chief of demons, the Satan, the enemy of God and of humankind; finally, there was a fascination with the names of angels. The historian Josephus (c.37–100), writing shortly after the time of Jesus, tells us that there was in his day a Jewish sect called the Essenes, who learnt and kept secret the names of angels. We know from Josephus and from the New Testament that there was another group of Jews, the Sadducees, who denied the existence of angels, but they seem to have been an exception. Most Jewish movements and most Jewish writings from the time of Jesus show a lively interest in angels.

After the birth of Jesus and the rise of Christianity, Jewish beliefs about angels continued to develop. This can be seen in the Talmud. The Talmud is a collection of books written by rabbis between 200 and 400 CE. Much of it is commentary on Scripture and reflections on Jewish case law. It contains a great deal about angels. Like the Septuagint, the Talmud often embellishes a scriptural tale by adding one or more angels. For example, when God creates a human being, the angels ask why God wishes to create such an odd creature. Again, it is angels who transfer the animals of Laban's flock to that of Jacob. The Talmud also adds details to the most famous story of angels, the hospitality of Abraham. According to the Talmud, the three angels who visited Abraham were Michael, Gabriel, and Raphael.

The fascination of the Essenes with the names of angels continues into the Middle Ages with an esoteric form of Judaism called Cabala (or Kabbalah), associated in particular, though not exclusively, with a collection of writings called the Zohar. Cabalistic writings not only contain many names of angels but also allege that these names can be used to conjure angels and to control all the powers and elements of nature. This takes us a long way from the unnamed strangers who visited Abraham and experienced his hospitality.

Angels in Christianity

Jesus was a Jew, and the first followers of Jesus were also Jews. Even after the Christian Church had separated from the rest of the Jewish community, the beliefs and practices of early Christianity were very much in continuity with Judaism. This is seen in relation to angels. Christian beliefs about angels are typical for Jews of their day.

There are two angels named in the New Testament: Gabriel, who announces to Mary that she will bear a son who will be the promised Messiah (Luke 1: 26–38), and Michael, who fights against the Devil (Jude 9; Revelation 12: 7). Both angels had already been named in the book of Daniel.

Jesus explicitly talked about angels a number of times and told his disciples that each child has an angel who 'continually sees the face of God' (Matthew 18: 10). In addition to the good angels, Jesus also spoke of demons and, in particular, of the Devil. Frequently Jesus 'cast out demons' from people who were 'possessed' and portrayed his mission as a war against demonic forces.

Paul, the first great missionary, who took the message of Christianity to the non-Jewish world, shared the same world view as Jesus. He presented the Christian life as a struggle against the Devil and against dark spiritual forces: 'principalities and powers' (Ephesians 6: 12). On the other hand, Paul was also ambivalent about angels. Paul warned people not to become fascinated by myths surrounding angels and demons. This could become a distraction from the true meaning of the gospel.

A parallel between Judaism and early Christianity is an interest in the hierarchy of different kinds of angels. In the fifth century, an anonymous Christian monk, writing under the name Dionysius, examined various scriptural passages and suggested there was a nine-level angelic hierarchy: angels, archangels, principalities, powers, virtues, dominations, thrones, cherubim, and seraphim. A similar theme is seen in later Jewish tradition, especially in the medieval Jewish thinker Moses Maimonides (1135–1204).

The Middle Ages saw a great interest in angels, as well as in prayers and rituals, in the art and architecture of the cathedrals, in the literature of Dante Alighieri (1265–1321), and among theologians. The most sustained attempt to understand angels was undertaken by Thomas Aquinas (1225–74).

He was a thinker of great genius, who continues to influence philosophy to this day. He wrote on many topics, but he was known as 'the angelic doctor' because of his much-loved work on angels.

The Middle Ages represent the high point of angelology—the systematic consideration of angels—but angels continued to inspire the Christian tradition in literature and art from John Milton (1608–74) to William Blake (1757–1827) to the present day.

Angels in Islam

Muslims are urged to 'follow the religion of Abraham' (Quran 3: 95) and all are duty bound to make pilgrimage (Hajj) to the shrine where, it is believed, Abraham stood to pray. Unsurprisingly, then, Islam shares the same stories and understanding of angels as those found in the other Abrahamic faiths: Judaism and Christianity.

The Quran makes reference to angels a number of times, not least to the 'honoured guests' who visited Abraham (51: 24). It also tells of the angels (in the plural) who visit Mary to tell her that she has been chosen from all women to be the mother of the Messiah, Jesus, son of Mary (3: 45). Like the New Testament, the Quran mentions by name the angels Gabriel and Michael (Jibril and Mikhail). Indeed, the revelation of the Quran is said to be transmitted by Gabriel (2: 97).

As well as the two angels named in the Hebrew Scriptures and the New Testament, the Quran also names two other angels: Harut and Marut. These teach the Babylonians about magic and sorcery.

A final supernatural creature, Iblis, is described in the Quran as the Devil (Shaitan). However, Iblis is not an angel but a 'djinn', a third kind of creature that is neither an angel nor a human being.

Belief in angels is one of the traditional 'six articles of belief' of Islam. In common with Christianity and Judaism, Islam emphasizes that angels are not gods but are servants of God who were created by God.

Angelic beings in Zoroastrianism and Hinduism

As mentioned above, the Jews developed their ideas about angels when they were in Babylon. The dominant religion of ancient Babylon was Zoroastrianism. There are some similarities between ancient Zoroastrian belief and Jewish belief about angels. For example, the idea of seven 'archangels', mentioned in the books of Tobit and Enoch, is sometimes said to echo the seven Amesha Spentas or divine sparks that give their names to the first seven days of the month in the Zoroastrian Calendar. Another example is the idea of 'guardian angels', which is said to be influenced by the guardian spirits (fravashis) of Zoroastrianism.

There are some parallels here, but we need to remember that Judaism and Zoroastrianism are very different religions. Zoroastrianism has some elements in common with Indian religion, and seems happy to speak about 'gods' in the plural. Jews believe fiercely that there is only one God. There are other differences. For example, the Zoroastrian concept of the fravashi is related to the soul. The fravashi is a part of the soul that remains in heaven. It is in some

11

ways like the personal daemon imagined in Philip Pullman's *Dark Materials* trilogy: less a distinct guardian spirit assigned to the person and more a reflection of the human spirit itself.

The parallels are also complicated by the fact that, under the influence of Christian missionaries in the nineteenth century, modern Zoroastrian doctrine has been presented in a way that is closer to Jewish and Christian teaching on angels. For example, the most common modern symbol for Zoroastrianism, a winged human figure (termed a faravahar because it is supposed to represent a fravashi), is in some ways a modern invention. Though the symbol is ancient, the name is modern. It seems likely that it originally represented the glory or dignity of the ruler and had nothing to do with angelic beings. There is no description of fravashi in the Zoroastrian Scriptures, and, if the faravahar symbol now seems like an angel, this is as much to do with modern Christian influence on Zoroastrianism as with ancient Zoroastrian influence on Judaism.

What is true for Zoroastrianism, which at least came into contact with Judaism, is even more true of Hinduism. There are, in Hinduism, creatures called devas and mahadevas, who are in some ways similar to angels and archangels. However, Hindu patterns of belief and practice are very different from those Judaism, Christianity, or Islam. The self and the world are understood differently, with the Hindu belief in a cycle of rebirth and souls that are in-between lives. Devas are sometimes said to be these in-between souls. At a more basic level, Hinduism and the Abrahamic religions seem to have different views on the relationship between the gods and the one

Figure 3 Faravahar is an ancient Zoroastrian symbol, but it came to represent an angelic being only in the nineteenth century.

God. In Hinduism, worship of many gods is compatible with belief in God. The gods are not rivals to the one God. The relationship is more subtle. In contrast, in Judaism, Christianity, and Islam, to worship 'other gods' is to turn away from the one God.

It is perhaps better not to use the word 'angel' for the spiritual creatures of Zoroastrianism or Hinduism. Drawing parallels between angels and fravashis, amesha spentas, devas or mahadevas, is more likely to confuse us than to enlighten us. These Zoroastrian and Hindu spirits do not play the same role in Zoroastrianism or Hinduism that angels play in Judaism, Christianity, and Islam. The word 'angel' and the contemporary imagery, ideas, and stories about angels have come down to us from a tradition that begins with Abraham. This book is about these beings. Hindu and Zoroastrian beliefs deserve books of their own.

Angels in Post-Christian Spirituality

Since the 1960s a spiritual movement has emerged that could be called post-Christian. It is typically ambivalent about established religion and seeks religious meaning through forms of religion that pre-date modern Christianity—for example, Celtic, Gnostic, or Pagan forms of religion. The historical distance between these ancient religions as they were practised and the present day is experienced not as a limitation but as a liberation, for it allows scope for the imagination. Symbols and ideas abstracted from their original context can become the focus of a newly reconstructed pattern of meaning and practice.

Angels are prominent in these post-Christian patterns of spirituality. This can be seen from the place of angels in the 'mind, body, spirit' section that exists in many high-street bookshops. Angels remain attractive because they appeal to the imagination and to personal experience. They are a non-threatening element from established religion. They seem not quite serious.

This raises an important question: does the content of these contemporary bookshelves bear any relationship to angels as they have been understood in Judaism, Christianity, or Islam? If it is confusing to call Zoroastrian fravashis 'angels', is it equally confusing to use the same word for new-age 'angels'?

There are differences between the angels of post-Christian spirituality and angels in the Abrahamic tradition. However, the new interest in angels certainly grows out of this older tradition. Books with titles such as *Angel Therapy* are shaped by ideas from Christianity and Judaism, even if the original context is no longer explicit. The very term 'angel' in English carries a great cultural heritage shaped by Christianity. Many of the doctrines found in these new-age writings are explicitly taken from Jewish sources, especially the Cabala. So it is appropriate to use the same word for these angels. Nevertheless, arguably these new-age books suffer from isolating the angels from their original context. The angels emerge from a particular tradition, an ancient tradition, a tradition that begins with Abraham sitting in the heat of the day by the oaks of Mamre.

2

Picturing Angels

Ancient Depictions of the Cherubim

The Ten Commandments in the Hebrew Scriptures include a very severe warning about carving images: 'You shall not make for yourself a graven image or any likeness of anything that is in heaven above, or that is in the earth beneath' (Exodus 20: 4). Nevertheless the same book describes how to carve two cherubim with wings facing one another to overshadow the 'mercy seat' to sit on top of the ark (Exodus 25: 20–1). This is nicely ironic, as the ark is the box that holds the tablets on which are written the Ten Commandments—which say you should not make images.

When Solomon built a temple to house the ark, in the sanctuary he placed two cherubim, each 10 cubits high with a 10 cubit wingspan—that is, around 17.5 feet (5.3 metres) high and the same distance across (1 Kings 6: 24). The wings of the cherubim were outstretched, so that the tip of one touched the wall and the tip of the other touched the other cherub. Unfortunately the ark was later lost (as any film-goer will know!). The ark was taken or hidden or destroyed when the Babylonians destroyed the Temple in

586 BCE. When the Temple was rebuilt after the exile there were no ark and no giant cherubim. It is, therefore, very difficult to know what the cherubim looked like. Some have imagined that cherubim looked like the winged bulls (the 'shedu') of the Assyrians or like a sphinx or a griffin (there is a scholarly theory that the words cherubim and griffin are related, but this is disputed). This idea is also based on the role of the cherubim as guards of the sanctuary. In other ancient cultures the shedu, griffin, or sphinx has this role.

The book of Ezekiel describes the cherubim as having wings outstretched and with faces of a man, an eagle, an ox, and a lion (Ezekiel 1: 10; see also Ezekiel 10: 14). However, Ezekiel does not say the cherubim have the body of an animal. Furthermore, the imagery of Ezekiel is deliberately exaggerated and may not reflect the Temple as it was. The other biblical accounts do not mention animal body parts in relation to cherubim. The cherubim on top of the ark face one another, and their wings 'overshadow' the mercy seat. This posture does not have parallels with images of shedu or other animal guards and Jewish writers from the third century CE suggest that these cherubs had human form (though not necessarily a human face).

It is certain that there were carved cherubim above the ark and in the sanctuary of Solomon's Temple before the exile (586 BCE), but unfortunately these were lost or destroyed centuries before Jesus was born, and no image of them remains. What is more, the descriptions in the Bible do not give a clear picture of what they looked like. According to Josephus, no one in his day knew what cherubim were supposed to look like. There is a break, then, between these ancient images of the cherubim and the images of angels painted by later artists.

Wings and Halos

The traditional depiction of angels has been shaped largely by Christian artists. This is in part because both in Judaism and in Islam there has been a reluctance to depict angels. Images of angels found in Islamic manuscripts from medieval Persia or in Ottoman culture, and the images of angels on Jewish amulets of the seventeenth century, are very much the exception and not the rule. The concern in both religions is that making sacred images can easily turn into worshipping images. The same concern over images has also led to some fierce disputes within Christianity. This flared up in the 'iconoclast' dispute in the eighth century in the Byzantine Empire and in the debate over statues and images in the sixteenth century in the Reformation in Britain and Germany. Thus in the East there are very few early icons that survived the iconoclast period, and in the West many statues, stained-glass windows and wall paintings were defaced, destroyed, or whitewashed. Nevertheless, the dominant forms of Christianity in East and West have allowed representational art, including sacred art. The history of depictions of angels is largely the history of Christian art and the art of those cultures shaped by Christianity.

The earliest depictions of angels are from the third century CE and are not in paintings or mosaics but are carved on objects and especially on sarcophagi. These show angels as young men without wings or halos, reflecting the biblical accounts of the angels who appeared to Abraham (Genesis 18: 2) or those who appeared to the women at the tomb of Jesus (Mark 16: 5). However, this begins to change even in the fourth century, when angels start to be depicted with wings. The particular way that winged angels are depicted at this time seems to be influenced by contemporary pagan images of the goddess Nike and the god Eros. Nevertheless, the idea that angels have wings was already well established among Christian and Jews.

In the Bible both the cherubim (Exodus 25: 20) and the seraphim (Isaiah 6: 2) have wings, and the psalmist imagines God like a charioteer, riding a cherub, and flying 'upon the wings of the wind' (2 Samuel 22: 11; Psalm 18: 10; Psalm 104: 3). By the time of Jesus it became common to believe that not only cherubim and seraphim but all spirits had wings. For example, the early Christian writer Tertullian (c.160–220) wrote that 'every spirit is winged, both angels and demons'. Similarly the Jewish Talmud describes both angels and demons as having wings with which they 'float from one end of the world to the other'.

Two centuries later, the Quran reiterates the claim that all angels have wings. 'Praise be to Allah . . . Who made the angel messengers with wings—two, or three, or four (pairs)' (35: 1) Compare this with the six-winged seraphim described in Isaiah (6: 2). This is not to say that angels are limited to three or four pairs. A tradition going back to the Hadith (the recorded sayings and deeds of the Prophet Muhammad) states that the archangels Gabriel and Michael each have 600 wings.

The Church of Santa Maria Maggiore in Rome has mosaics that date from the early fifth century. There are scenes of the

Figure 4 *The fifth-century mosaics in the church of Santa Maria Maggiore show angels with wings and halos.*

events surrounding the birth of Jesus that include many angels. These angels are young men dressed in white Roman togas. They are instantly recognizable as angels to a twenty-first-century observer, and show the archetypal image of an angel with a white gown (on the white garment see, for example, Matthew 28: 3 and Mark 16: 5) with wings and a halo.

It is interesting that, at this early stage, Jesus is depicted with a halo, but not Mary or Joseph. The halo is associated with the glory of God in Jesus in particular and not yet with the saints. The halo was an artistic device taken from pagan culture. It was used in ancient Greece and Rome before the time of Jesus to show the gloriousness of a god. Halos were sometimes also used in depictions of the emperor as a mark of his power and his semi-divine status. It is probably this use that is applied by Christians to depictions of Jesus and then to the angels, who are witnesses and companions to Jesus. The angel's halo is a visual link with the halo of Jesus and shows that the angel is present because of Jesus.

The standard image of an angel as a man with wings and usually also a halo has endured from the fifth century to the present day. It has been sufficiently common to be recognizable to Christians of different traditions in different cultures separated by many centuries. In the early Middle Ages one partial exception to this rule was the portrayal of 'tetramorphic' creatures inspired by the visions of Ezekiel (chapter 10) and Revelation (chapter 4). These were sometimes portrayed as four separate creatures (often representing the four gospels) but sometimes were portrayed as a single four-headed creature. They occur both in the Byzantine East and in the Latin West and may represent cherubim or seraphim or may sometimes be imagined as a third kind of winged spiritual being. However, they became much less common after the Renaissance, and the human winged figure remains the dominant image.

Heavenly Harps

Nowhere in the Hebrew Scriptures or in the New Testament or in the Quran are angels portrayed playing harps. However, both in the New Testament (Revelation 8: 2) and in the Quran (39: 68) an angel is portrayed blowing a trumpet to announce the end of time and the last judgement. It is not surprising, then, that early images of angels tended to show them without musical instruments, and when an instrument was shown it was likely to be a horn or a trumpet. Nevertheless, there is a clear link between angels and music. Several of the psalms enjoin the praise of God, and one in particular (Psalm 148) urges the angels to this:

> Praise the Lord from the heavens
> Praise him in the heights!
> Praise him, all his angels
> Praise him, all his host!

In the gospel story angels are seen praising God the night that Jesus is born: 'And suddenly there was with the angel a multitude of the heavenly host praising God' (Luke 2: 13). Similarly, in Isaiah (6: 3) and in the book of Revelation (4: 8) the six winged seraphim never cease to sing, 'Holy, holy, holy, is the Lord God Almighty'.

In human worship, the praise of God is associated with making music:

> Raise a song, sound the timbrel,
> the sweet lyre with the harp.
> Blow the trumpet at the new moon
> at the full moon, on our feast day.
>
> (Psalm 81: 2–3; see also Psalm 33: 2,
> 57: 8, 71: 22 and 92: 3)

This becomes a popular motif in the West from the twelfth century onwards. Angels are shown playing every kind of musical instrument—lutes, flutes, viols, mandoras, horns, and drums, as well as harps. In fact, the depiction of angels is a very important resource for the history of music. Generations of artists portrayed angels with the kinds of musical instruments that were prevalent in their day. In the fifteenth century, on an altarpiece by Jan van Eyck, the angels are even seen reading music. Before this time the angels presumably played by ear.

The strong popular association of angels with harps in particular does not seem to originate from the traditional artistic representation of angels. It probably stems from a verse in the book of Revelation where the saints in heaven are shown 'with harps of God in their hands' (Revelation 15: 2; see also Revelation 14: 2). It is saints who get harps when they die, and angels are associated with harps because of a popular confusion of angels with the saints in heaven. The stereotype of the angel with the harp is probably very recent, perhaps as recent as the nineteenth century (though the reader may find earlier examples). Before this, however, angels are associated with music-making in general, with the praise of God, and also with the harmony of the universe, 'the song of the spheres'.

From Icons to Naturalism and Back

The representation of angels follows the same progression as the history of Christian art more generally. This is a rich and complex history.

The earliest style to develop is that of ancient Rome before the time of Constantine (*c*.272–337). This is found on the walls and sarcophagi of the catacombs. Angels played relatively little role in this early art, and where they were present they were inconspicuous figures without wings.

With the declaration of religious toleration by Constantine in 313 CE it became possible to build large public churches and decorate them with frescos and mosaics. This setting also encouraged a more confident portrayal of Christianity and, in particular, of Christ in majesty as judge of the world. This change of focus in part explains the shift towards the portrayal of angels in heaven, including the portrayal of cherubim and seraphim. In this context it became common to portray all angels with wings and halos, as seen, for example, in the mosaics in the Church of Santa Maria Maggiore.

At this period the styles of art of Eastern and Western Christianity were very similar, as they shared a common ancient Roman culture. A divergence started with the collapse of the Roman Empire in the West and with a subsequent mixing of Roman culture with the more primitive aesthetics of various tribes: the Celts, Franks, and Goths. This mixing lies at the roots of the medieval art of the West. In contrast, the Greek-speaking Eastern part of the Roman Empire continued with its capital in Constantinople (also known as Byzantium) until the fall of that city to the Turks in 1453 CE.

In the Byzantine East the style of Christian art that was developed in the fifth century came to be thought of as uniquely sacred. This may have been a result of the fierce 'iconoclastic' disputes over the veneration of images. It led to a view that a sacred icon should have a very particular style. At a deeper level this very conservative aesthetic may also reflect the desire of Byzantium to preserve a classical culture that had been lost in the West. From the perspective of a later age, Byzantine art is sometimes held to have a symbolic focus and not to be so concerned with realistic representation. The faces of Christ and of Mary could be portrayed in a very realistic way, but other figures, and especially angels, tended to be presented as flat and stylized, albeit in gold or a brilliant colour. With the spread of Orthodox Christianity, the Byzantine style influenced iconography in Bulgaria, Greece, and Russia. It is evident, for example, in the work of Andrei Rublev.

Early medieval art in the West was initially less technically proficient and less sophisticated than Byzantine art, but had in common with Byzantine art the emphasis on symbol and communication, with less emphasis on the search for accurate representation. This was shown, for example, by the use of halos and by the use of characteristic items (sword, key, palm, and so on) to identify different saints and angels.

This pattern begins to break down with the work of Giotto di Bondone (1267–1337) in the early fourteenth century. While still working in the medieval tradition, Giotto developed a much more naturalist style, with accurate portrayal of posture and a sense of depth and movement in his pictures. In the fifteenth century Western artists discovered how to paint using perspective, and painters in Northern Europe and in Italy increasingly attempt a naturalistic style. Jan van Eyck (*c*.1395–1441) dispensed with halos, as this would have detracted from the realism of his paintings. An altar piece in Ghent shows the angel Gabriel with wings but with no halo, while another altarpiece depicts a group of angels singing wearing ornate cloaks but with neither halos nor wings (unless the wings are supposed to be hidden under the cloaks) (see Fig. 13 on p. 99).

At this time John of Fiesole (*c*.1400–55), a Dominican friar, was painting churches and priories. He received the nickname 'Fra Angelico', not only because he painted angels but also because of his saintly manner of life. In 1982 he was recognized as a saint (technically a 'blessed'—a kind of minor saint) by Pope John Paul II and in 1984 he was named patron of the arts. Fra Angelico was somewhat conservative in style and exceptional in his day in nearly always painting saints with halos and angels with wings and halos.

At the turn of the sixteenth century, the Renaissance reaches the height of its technical brilliance. It is interesting that two of the masters of the high Renaissance, Raphael Sanzio (1483–1520) and Michelangelo Buonarroti (1475–1564), were both named after angels. With these painters the natural expression of form, posture, colour, and emotion were perfected to such a degree that the art itself, rather than the religious subject matter, seemed to have become the real focus. The angelic images of this period were realistic portrayals of young men or children, except with wings.

The spirit of the Renaissance was overtaken by a shockwave that hit Western Europe in the sixteenth century: the religious upheaval of the Protestant Reformation and the Catholic Counter-Reformation (perhaps better termed the Catholic Reformation). This upheaval had a direct effect on the portrayal of angels.

The Protestant Reformers were to a greater or lesser extent suspicious of the cult of angels and saints and the use of religious images. They favoured a simpler form of religion focused on the Bible and on the person of Jesus. In this context, art and painting did not die out but looked to more secular and domestic themes. Artists in Protestant lands typically painted portraits for private homes rather than religious images for churches, and there was a decline in the depiction of angels.

At the same time, in Catholic Countries there was a parallel Catholic Reformation inspired by the Council of Trent (1545–63). In addition to looking at doctrine and church order, this Council directly considered the question of Christian art. The Council encouraged religious art but criticized profane or pagan influences, nudity, and disorderliness. The Catholic Reformation created a style of art and architecture called baroque, which was confident, ornate, and very explicitly religious. This effectively ended more primitive forms of medieval art and iconography still popular until that time. The art of the baroque is more emotionally expressive than the Renaissance, which reflected the calm classical art of ancient Greece and Rome. A good example of the expression of passion in baroque art is *The Ecstasy of Saint Teresa* by Giovanni Bernini (1598–1680). This statue depicts a sixteenth-century nun, Teresa of Avilla (1515–82), being pierced through the heart by an angel. The scene is highly emotional, indeed erotic, but it is also explicitly religious.

In the eighteenth century the inspiration behind baroque art was succeeded by a more domestic style called Rococo. This was a popular time for those most frivolous of angels, the fat-faced cherubs or putti. Despite the efforts of the Catholic Reformation, this period also saw a rise in what have been called 'secular angels'. The image of the cherub continued to be used interchangeably in Christian art and pagan allegory. When putti were used as domestic decoration without explicit religious context, it was difficult to say whether it had any religious content.

Interest in angels was revived in diverse and interesting ways in the nineteenth century, which saw a romantic reaction against the Industrial Revolution and an artistic reaction against the continuing influence of the high Renaissance. This was seen in particular in the work of William Blake early in the century and later in a movement that called itself the Pre-Raphaelite Brotherhood. The Pre-Raphaelites sought to recapture the direct and heartfelt character of early Renaissance and medieval art and rejected art that was conventional or formulaic. They often painted angels.

While the Pre-Raphaelites and other nineteenth-century movements rejected the conventional forms of art of their day, they continued to be attentive to nature and to natural forms. In the twentieth century this last convention was also broken with the rise of abstract art. Yet even within this most modern artistic context the idea of angels continued to haunt the imagination. A good example is provided by Paul Klee (1879–1940). He was a friend and associate of Wassily Kandinsky (1866–1944), the most influential of all abstract artists. As Klee was dying, he drew and painted a number of angels. They are crude line drawings with titles such as 'still ugly', 'incomplete', 'applicant', and 'forgetful angel' (see Fig. 8 on p. 50). The angel represents a spiritual meaning that is hard to capture in a harsh modern world on the eve of the Second World War. The few lines evoke the idea, while the lack of definition, colour, or beauty is part of the meaning of the picture. Klee's angels abstract all beauty from the angels of Raphael or Michelangelo, and yet the incomplete and forgetful angels remain as a token of hope.

The most difficult thing about writing this book has been the need to exclude so many different representations of angels. I would expect all readers will know of some representation of an angel they would have liked to see reproduced here. Like the angels themselves, the images of angels are almost uncountable.

One last point of reference I will give was created by the sculptor Antony Gormley (1950–) at the end of the twentieth century. The *Angel of the North* in Gateshead in the north of England stands 66 feet (20 metres) tall, with wings measuring 178 feet (54 metres) across: a wingspan wider than the Statue of Liberty is tall. It was cast from 200 tonnes of steel, an industrial angel to celebrate an area whose greatness had once been based on heavy industry. Like Klee's angel, the *Angel of the North* is immediately recognizable, though the form is very simple, with no facial features, no halo, and with wings for arms. There is in these twentieth-century representations a return from naturalism to the symbolic. The *Angel of the North* is iconic.

From Cherubim to Putti

It is difficult to know exactly how people in ancient Israel imagined the cherubim. But it is certain that they were formidable creatures. The first mention of cherubim is as guards who block the way back to paradise, together with a burning fiery sword (Genesis 3: 24). The statues of the cherubim in the Temple were over 17 feet (5.2 metres) high (1 Kings 6: 24).

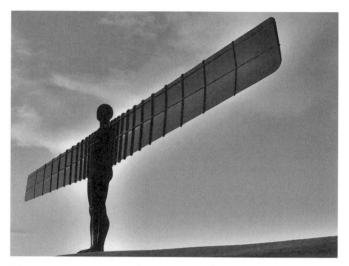

Figure 5 The *Angel of the North* is iconic, an angel cast in steel for an industrial region.

They are described by Ezekiel as having four heads and many eyes and wings (Ezekiel 10), the tetramorphic monster of Byzantine art. How did these fierce creatures become the 'little cherubs' that we think of today—fat children with tiny wings and a smirk on their face?

The story starts in antiquity with depictions of the god Eros (in Greece) or Cupid (in Rome) as a winged boy with a bow and arrow. Eros was the child of Venus and had the power to make people fall in love. Often he was presented as mischievous or fickle. Associated with Eros were lesser gods or messengers called Erotes or Cupids. These were also represented as naked boys with wings and were often shown gathering grapes for a feast. They were associated with the cult of Dionysius (also called Bacchus), the god of wine, and thus with the portrayal of ritual 'Bacchic feasts'.

In the second and third century CE it became common to decorate sarcophagi with images of Erotes. This practice seems to have begun for the burial of children but later was also used for adults. From very early it seems that Christians assimilated this imagery. For example, one sarcophagus of the period shows a bearded man carrying a sheep on his shoulder while winged boys gather grapes. This could be Bacchus surrounded by Erotes or it could be Christ, the good shepherd, surrounded by angels.

While it seems certain that early Christians used Erotes images to portray angels, this had little influence on Christian art after Constantine, either in the Byzantine East or in the early Medieval West. The figure of the child angel was rather 'rediscovered' by Italian artists in the Renaissance. If there is one artist who is credited with reinventing the figure of the child angel it is Donatello (1386–1466). He was part of a larger revival of classical culture seen in art and architecture. It runs parallel to Renaissance humanism with its interest in Greek and classical Latin eloquence. These winged children were called 'putti' (meaning little men) and were used in Christian paintings to portray angels but also in paintings of Greek myths. Often there was nothing to distinguish these images except the context. In a Christian context they were angels, in a Greek mythic context they were cupids.

The identification of winged boys with angels goes back to antiquity and was revived by Donatello, but at this point they were not yet identified with the cherubim. It is unclear precisely when this happens or why, but it seems to have happened by the late Renaissance, as is evident from the following extraordinary passage from the diary of Teresa of Avila.

I saw an angel close by me, on my left side, in bodily form ... He was not large, but small of stature, and most beautiful—his face burning, as if he were one of the highest angels, who seem to be all of fire: they must be those whom we call cherubim. Their names they never tell me; but I see very well that there is in heaven so great a difference between one angel and another, and between these and the others, that I cannot explain it. I saw in his hand a long spear of gold, and at the iron's point there seemed to be a little fire. He appeared to me to be thrusting it at times into my heart and to pierce my very entrails; when he drew it out, he seemed to draw them out also, and to leave me all on fire with a great love of God. The pain was so great, that it made me moan; and yet so surpassing was the sweetness of this excessive pain, that I could not wish to be rid of it.

The image of the boylike angel with the golden spear very obviously evokes the image of the god Eros or Cupid. The experience is religious, but it is described in deliberately erotic terms. Bernini's statue of Teresa expresses a passion that is already evident in this writing. Teresa identified the angel as a cherub precisely because cherubim were the highest angels in the Christian hierarchy of angels. They were the ones closest to God and hence they represented for Teresa the burning love of God.

The putti were childlike but they were not innocent. They were wise and knowing. For this reason they were sometimes portrayed with adult faces—an effect that can be

Figure 6 Bernini's statue of Teresa in ecstasy shows a cherub looking like Eros, the Greek god of love.

quite disturbing. As secular images they represented romantic love, levity, and earthly happiness; as sacred images they represented divine love and heavenly bliss. The baroque deliberately traded on this ambiguity, mixing earthly and heavenly imagery. However, the image of the cherub, so often a figure of fun, has become so trivial that it has lost its ability to express religious meaning, at least in Western Europe. It can no longer express the baroque confidence in the closeness of heaven or the passionate mysticism of Teresa or Bernini. This is why the nineteenth century turned away from the putto and sought to show, in the words of Rilke (1875–1926), that 'every angel is terrifying' because 'beauty is nothing but the beginning of terror'.

From Male to Female

One final question in relation to the depiction of angels relates to the sex of angels. Are they male, female, or sexless? When the angels appear to Abraham, they are described as 'three men' (Genesis 18: 2). So also when Mary Magdalene sees an angel, his appearance is of 'a young man dressed in a white robe' (Mark 16: 5). The names of the angels that appear in Jewish literature (Gabriel, Michael, Raphael, and so on) are all masculine in form, and the earliest Christian images are clearly masculine. This is all the more striking if, as art historians argue, the typical Christian representation of a winged angel was influenced by the image of the goddess of victory, Nike.

In Christian iconography the Archangel Michael is typically represented in military uniform, and this is sometimes also true of other angels. The heavenly host is the spiritual army of God. This has the effect of reinforcing the male imagery.

Jesus says of the angels that they do not marry (Matthew 22: 30), and it is the standard Christian view that they are pure spirits without bodies (Hebrews 1:14; compare with Luke 24: 39). This would seem to imply that angels are neither male nor female. Nevertheless, the portrayal of angels in early Christian iconography is exclusively male.

A similar pattern is found in Islam. The common opinion of scholars in Islam is that angels do not marry and that they are neither male nor female. On the other hand, the Quran states that, 'had we sent an angel, we would have sent him in the form of a man' (6: 9), and seems to condemn the view that angels are female: 'Did we create the angels to be females?' (37: 150; see also 43: 19). Hence, while in reality angels are neither male nor female, their appearance is always male.

The Renaissance saw not only the representation of angels like children (putti) but also an increasing tendency towards portraying angels as androgynous or effeminate. The historian Henry Mayr-Harting links this development with a shift from seeing angels as intervening on earth in the social sphere, bolstering the power of kings and of providing an occult power used by sorcerers, to seeing angels as benign and well-ordered beings whose activity was safely focused in heaven, with the contemplation of God. He calls this the 'aetherialisation' of angels. It should also be noticed that Renaissance artists looked as much to classical Greek sources for their inspiration as they did to the Bible. The young men who visit Abraham had to compete in the artists' imagination with the feminine figures of Nike and the Muses.

The high point of this process of feminization came in the nineteenth century and was strongly associated with the Romantic Movement. Whereas in the Middle Ages angels had been thought of as pure intellects, in the nineteenth century they were thought of as representing the imagination. Angels became elements in a romantic vision that was now only loosely attached to the Christian tradition. In this context, angels were portrayed not as androgynous but clearly as young women, and it is these nineteenth-century images that shape contemporary popular culture.

Thus, if someone is described as 'an angel' in a modern context, the typical cultural assumption is that the person is a woman. That is why the all-female detective agency of the American 1970s TV series was called *Charlie's Angels* and why the British TV series of the same era about student nurses was called *Angels*. This tendency has its exceptions in film and other popular media, but in post-Christian society the portrayal of angels remains predominantly feminine. This gradual shift from male to female also seems to confirm the suggestion of the feminist thinker Michele Le Doeuff, that once some category becomes devalued and loses its grand philosophical status then it starts to become regarded as feminine. Angels are as popular as ever, but they are not so intellectually respectable as they once were. As they are taken less seriously and command less cultural respect, so men portray them as female.

3

What is an Angel?

Not Little Gods but Spiritual Creatures

Angels are not little gods. This is an important point about angels. It is what distinguishes belief in angels from polytheism, which has a pantheon of gods with Zeus or Jupiter as the 'top god'. Angels belong to religions that have only one God, but where God has spiritual servants, messengers, courtiers, or soldiers. These are creatures and have a place within the created order and a role in the plan of the Creator. In the Hebrew Scriptures the angels may sometimes be described as the 'sons of God' (for example Job 1: 6), but Jewish, Christian, and Islamic theologians all agree that angels are spiritual *creatures*. They are not eternal or equal to God.

The Abrahamic religions proclaim that there is one God who created the heavens and the earth. The universe is a cosmos, an ordered whole, created with a divine purpose. Some other religions have seen the beginning of the world as the result of a battle between warring gods, or as an accident. This is not the case with Judaism, Christianity, and Islam. These traditions hold that the world was created on purpose and that everything in it was created by God. There was no one else with God before creation. If we imagine a line between God and everything God created, then angels are on this side of the line with human beings, rabbits, trees, stars, and everything else in the world.

Some historians argue that belief in angels represents a compromise with polytheism. They say that ancient Judaism was not as strongly monotheistic as it later became. We saw earlier how Zoroastrian belief seems to have influenced Judaism, at least in giving the angels names. It is hard to know exactly what people believed in ancient Israel, but certainly by the time of the Maccabean revolt Jews were notorious for worshipping only one God. Indeed, Romans and Greeks regarded Jews as fanatical for this very reason. And yet, at the same time as the Jews were asserting their monotheism, they were also becoming more interested in angels.

When were Angels Created?

There is common agreement, among those who believe in angels, that angels were created. There is much less agreement about precisely when angels were created. In the book of Genesis, there are two accounts of creation: in the first the world is made in six days (Genesis 1: 2–2: 3); in the second the first human being (Adam) is moulded from clay and then God breathes into his nostrils the breath of life (Genesis 2: 7). The Quran also states that God created the world in six days (7: 54, 10: 3, 11: 7, 25: 59) and that Adam was created out of clay (15: 26, 32: 7). According to a Hadith, Muhammad said that Adam was created on the last day, the Friday. This agrees with the Hebrew account. Thus the main outline, at least, of the story of the creation of human beings is common to Jews, Christians, and Muslims. However, neither in the Hebrew Scriptures nor in the Quran is there an explicit story about how and when the angels were created. It should also be noted that one's whole approach to this question will also depend on how one interprets the sacred text. Are these passages of Scripture to be understood literally, or as allegory, or in some other way?

In Judaism (in the Talmud) and in Islam (in the Quran) the angels are said to be present when God creates the first human beings. In the Talmud the angels ask God what he is doing. In the Quran they are invited to bow down and honour this new creation (which the angels do, but Iblis refuses to do). These stories imply that the angels were created before human beings, but it is not clear how long before. In the Talmud some rabbis say that angels were created on the second day, to make it clear that the angels were not around from the beginning and did not help with the creation. Other rabbis pushed it forward to the fifth day, the day before human beings were created. One very early Muslim Scholar, Al-Tabari (838–870), argued that angels were created early on the sixth day and that Adam was created later the same day. None of these speculations has any great weight in the Jewish or Islamic tradition.

Christians have generally placed the creation of angels at the beginning of the works of creation. The Hebrew Scriptures begin with the words: 'In the begining God created the

Figure 7 In the Quran the angels bow down to worship God.

heavens and the earth' (Genesis 1: 1). By the fourth century CE Christians were expressing their faith in 'God, the Father Almighty, maker of heaven and earth, of all things visible and invisible' (Creed of Nicea, 325 CE). 'The heavens' came to be understood as 'all things invisible', including the angels, whereas 'the earth' was understood as 'all things visible'— that is, the whole of the material creation. This is made even more explicit at an important Church council held in the Middle Ages: 'Creator of all things invisible and visible, spiritual and corporeal . . . angelic, namely, and worldly, and then human, as it were, common, composed of spirit and body' (Creed of Lateran IV, 1215 CE).

There was, however, an ancient difference of opinion among Christians about when precisely the angels were created. Some Greek-speaking Christians said that angels were created before the material universe, others, mainly Latin-speaking Christians, said that angels were created at the same time as the material universe. Thomas Aquinas argued that the Latin opinion made more sense, for angels do not constitute a universe all of their own; they and the material world together make one cosmos. But he recognized that the answer to this question is not clear, either from the Scriptures or from natural reason. So he was not willing to say that people who held the Greek view were wrong. There is a consensus among Jewish, Christian, and Islamic theologians that angels were created and that they were created before the first human beings were created. However, there is no consensus in any tradition about precisely when the angels were created. It is not revealed.

What are Angels Made from?

If angels were made, what were they made out of? What kind of bodies do they have?

According to the Talmud, the essence of the angels is fire. They were made from fire and are sustained by fire. In the Hebrew Scriptures, in one of the psalms the Lord 'makes the winds his messengers, fire and flame his ministers' (Psalm 104: 4). Another possible source of this idea may be the angel who speaks to Moses from the burning bush (Exodus 3: 2) or maybe the burning fiery chariot that takes Elijah to heaven (2 Kings 2: 11). Fire has also been associated, in the Jewish tradition, with prayer and sacrifice, with burnt offerings. There is an interesting story in the book of Judges when an angel appears to Gideon. Gideon brings the angel some meat, bread, and soup. However, unlike the angels who appeared to Abraham, this angel does not eat the food. Rather he asks Gideon to put the food on a rock. The angel then touches the food with his staff and it bursts into flame (Judges 6: 19–22).

Fire is associated with light and heat. It travels upwards, towards heaven. It is not heavy, as human bodies are. Nevertheless, angels do not always appear in fiery form, and another theory expressed in the Talmud is that angels are made from a mixture of fire and water, with God preventing these two elements from consuming each other.

Islamic belief is expressed in a well-known Hadith: 'The angels are created from light, just as the djinn are created from smokeless fire and mankind is created from what you have been told about [that is, from clay].' In Islam it is not angels but djinn who were made of fire. Angels were made from the most sublime of elements, from light itself. There is an interesting parallel here between the teaching of Islam and the writings of the great Christian theologian Augustine of Hippo (a town in North Africa) (354–430). Augustine argued that the angels were created when God said 'let there be light' (Genesis 1: 3). The angels are 'light' because the light of God shines on them. God is the eternal light. God is all wisdom and understanding and love. The angels were created to share in and to reflect this light. We use the word 'seeing' to mean not only seeing visible objects but also 'seeing the point', understanding something. In the same way, 'light' can mean not just light that makes things visible but the light of understanding. According to Augustine, this explains why God created angels by using the words 'let there be light'.

Saying that angels are essential fire, or that they are made from light, helps to distinguish angels from human beings and other animals. Human beings and other animals are from the earth and our bodies will return to the earth. Angels do not have the kind of bodies that human beings have. They are heavenly not earthly. So far so good, but it seems that we get into difficulties if we imagine that angels are made of ordinary fire, which is not even an element but a state of matter. If there are difficulties thinking that angels are made from physical fire, there are worse difficulties thinking that angels are made from particles of visible light. Light is not a kind of material; in the terms of modern physics, it has no 'rest mass'. Are we to imagine that each kind of angel has a specific temperature (of fire) or a specific wavelength (of light)? In an important sense, angels are part of the 'unseen' world. They cannot be understood the way that physical bodies are understood. There is no physics of angels. It can be helpful even today to say that angels are made from fire or from light, but only if we realize that this is a metaphorical way of speaking. It is a way of saying that angels are real but they do not have material bodies.

In the Middle Ages of the Common Era a distinctively philosophical approach to thinking about angels emerged in each of the three Abrahamic faiths. This tradition had its roots in the philosophy of Plato (429–347 BCE) and Aristotle (384–322 BCE), but it was transmitted and reshaped by Jewish, Muslim, and Christian influences. It is this tradition that is found, *par excellence*, in the works of Thomas Aquinas. According to this way of thinking, angels are spiritual creatures with intellect and will, but they do not have bodies of any kind.

Philosophers and Angels

According to Plato, the human soul is something essentially immaterial that pre-exists the body and is better off if it can escape the body. At death, depending on how the person has lived, the soul will either escape from the body or go into another body. If the person has been wicked, then, in the next life, the soul might enter the body of an irrational animal—a hawk or a wolf. Plato also believed that between human beings and the gods were intermediate beings called 'daimons' who could inspire human thoughts and actions. These daimons were greater than ordinary human beings but less than gods. They might be the spirits of dead heroes. The idea of the daimon seems to pre-date Plato, but after his time it became more widespread and was discussed by many philosophers.

Plato's most brilliant student, Aristotle, did not share Plato's view that the soul was better off without the body. He thought that the soul made sense only as the life of a living body. He was very vague about where the intellectual part of the human soul came from or what happened to it after death. Many followers of Aristotle explicitly denied the immortality of the soul. On the other hand, Aristotle shared with Plato the idea that there are creatures with intelligence that do not have bodies. Aristotle argued that the stars and the planets are moved by these incorporeal intelligences.

Plato's ideas had a strong influence on a Jewish philosopher called Philo of Alexandria (*c.*20 BCE–50 CE), who lived in Alexandria in Egypt. Philo looked for parallels between Greek ideas and the Hebrew Scriptures. On the subject of angels he wrote: 'the beings whom other philosophers called daimons, Moses usually called angels.' He also believed that 'souls, demons, and angels differ in name but they are identical in reality'. Philo seems to have accepted Plato's picture of a cycle of reincarnation with souls rising or falling, becoming angels or becoming demons.

Two hundred years later, Origen (*c.*185–254), another resident of Alexandria, introduced these same ideas into the Christian tradition. Origen also believed that human souls, angels, and demons are the same kind of thing. He thought that, at the beginning of time, every soul was given a choice, and those who chose well became angels, and those who chose less well became human, and those who made bad choices became demons. Origen also believed that this was not just a one-off decision. In the future a human being might become an angel or a demon, and an angel might fall and become a demon. He also thought that at least some demons might make good choices and become angels. Origen was very controversial, and some of his ideas were rejected. He seemed to his contemporaries to be arguing for a version of reincarnation, an idea that would contradict the Christian Scriptures.

Augustine was influenced both by Plato and by Origen. He strongly defended the idea that human beings have a soul that is spiritual and immortal. He believed that, if people reflected on their experience and looked inward, each person would realize that he or she was not only a physical being. Augustine's views changed during his career as he reflected more deeply on things. In some ways Augustine was more critical of Plato than Origen had been. Augustine realized that Plato had not given enough respect to the human body. In opposition to this, Augustine came to stress that human beings are very different from angels. Origen thought that some souls became human and some souls became angels. He thought that angels had bodies, of a very light and subtle kind. Augustine argued that human souls and angels were different in kind. Human beings were a unity of body and soul, but angels had no body at all. They were pure spirits and were created that way. They had no need for a body. Augustine's view became the predominant Christian view and was developed by Aquinas. Nevertheless, some later Christians retained

Origen's view that angels have bodies of a subtle kind. This was the view of Milton, for example.

After the time of Augustine the influence of Plato gradually became less dominant, and people found more inspiration in the philosophy of Aristotle. This happened in all three of the Abrahamic traditions: Judaism, Christianity, and Islam. Christian Aristotelianism can be traced back to Boethius (c.480–525). However, it did not flower until the thirteenth century, when the works of Aristotle were rediscovered through contacts with the Islamic world. The most important Islamic Aristotelian was the great Persian polymath Ibn Sina, known in the West as Avicenna (c.980–1037). He exercised a great influence over Islamic, Jewish, and Christian thinkers, including Moses Maimonides and Thomas Aquinas. All these thinkers attempted to combine Aristotle's philosophy with a world view taken from their sacred Scriptures. Thus they interpreted the 'pure intelligences' of Aristotle's system as being the angels of God.

In his famous *Guide for the Perplexed*, Maimonides said:

We have already stated above that the angels are incorporeal. This agrees with the opinion of Aristotle: there is only this difference in the names employed—he uses the term 'Intelligences,' and we say instead 'angels'. His theory is that the Intelligences are intermediate beings between the Prime Cause and existing things, and that they effect the motion of the spheres, on which motion the existence of all things depends. This is also the view we meet with in all parts of Scripture: every act of God is described as being performed by angels.

This passage was quoted with approval by Thomas Aquinas. It is worth pausing to consider how, at this point in time, there was a positive interaction between Jewish, Islamic, and Christian writers. It was a time when there were great tensions between their communities, with outbreaks of hostility, persecution, and armed struggle. Yet the greatest minds within each community acknowledged their debt to one another, and a symbol of this is the common tradition on angels.

Among Islamic, Jewish, and Christian writers there was a common wish to combine philosophy and faith. They used Aristotle, who was a pagan, a non-believer, but provided the best philosophical understanding of the world then available. They combined this with a vision of life provided by the sacred Scriptures: the Quran or the Bible. They held in common a belief in angels as God's messengers and common stories about angels in their Scriptures. What follows will rely in particular on Thomas Aquinas. He acknowledged his debt to Ibn Sina and to 'the Rabbi Moses' (Maimonides). Nevertheless, it is Thomas Aquinas himself who produced the most well-developed and sustained account, indeed the single most influential account, there has ever been of the nature of an angel.

Pure Spirits without Bodies

In his treatise on angels, Thomas Aquinas started with the question: 'Are the angels completely without bodies?' He wrote that, in the ancient world, many people thought that nothing existed except what they could see and feel—physical bodies. In our day this ancient attitude is back in fashion, at least with some people. The successes of the physical sciences and of modern technology seem to show that all that matters essentially is the physical world that we can weigh and measure.

Thomas Aquinas pointed out that, even when we are thinking about material things, our thoughts are not themselves physical. If we know that snow is white and cold, that knowledge is not white or cold. When I think of snow, the snow is physically not in my head. We might say 'the thought is in my head', but this is not really true either—thoughts refer to physical objects, but they are not physical objects. My wife is always in my thoughts, but she is not, literally, in my head.

There can be realities that are not physical objects. We are more comfortable thinking about things that we can touch and hold and see. Even very big things (like galaxies) and very small things (like atoms) are difficult for us to think about. They make us feel dizzy if we try to imagine them. It is even more difficult for us to think about things that are not physical at all, like numbers or moral principles. Thus it is not easy for us to think about what it is to have conscious thoughts—to reflect on our own awareness. Yet we know that consciousness is something real, that we are conscious, and that other people are too.

According to Thomas Aquinas, angels are also real, though they are not physical. Human beings have physical properties (like being tall or bald or having a cold) and have non-physical properties (like being intelligent or forgiving or thinking about snow). Angels have no bodies, so they have no physical properties. Human beings have a life cycle. We are born and

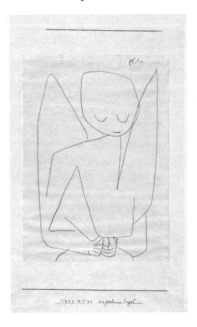

Figure 8 Paul Klee's *Forgetful Angel* (*Vergesslicher Engel*) is forgetful of his angelic nature but still exists somehow.

we die. We eat to survive. When we eat, stuff goes into us, and when we breathe or sweat or go to the toilet, stuff comes out of us. We distinguish ourselves from each other by who our parents were and where we were born or brought up and what we do, but we also share a common humanity. If angels have no bodies, then none of this is true of angels. Angels are not born and do not die. They do not eat. They neither get fat nor lose weight. They have no weight. No angel is taller than another angel.

How, then, can you tell two angels apart? This was a real problem for Thomas Aquinas. He thought that what distinguished two human beings was to do with their physical life—ultimately I am over here and you are over there and this is my body and that is yours. This led him to say something rather mysterious—that there can only be one angel of each species. All human beings share the same species—every human being has human parents. However, angels have no parents and they are not born in a particular place. They are not distinguished by the history of their bodies.

Does this mean that there is only one angel—who rushes around like Beau Geste to create the impression that he is a large army? Thomas Aquinas accepted the common view of Jews, Christians, and Muslims that there was a great number of angels. His solution was to say that every one of these angels is specifically different. There are as many species of angels as there are angels. Just as there are millions of species of insects, so there are still more species of angel, 'far beyond all material multitude'.

Angels do not have bodies, but they often appear to have bodies. For example, the three angels who visited Abraham sat down and shared a meal. Thomas Aquinas responded that, in order to be seen, angels sometimes took on a material body that they made from condensed air. This looks like a human body, but it is not a living body. It is more like a puppet moved by the angel. For this reason Aquinas argued that angels could not really eat or drink. When the angels visited Abraham, they did not truly eat. In support of this Thomas quoted from the book of Tobit, where the angel says: 'When I was with you I seemed indeed to eat and drink, but you were seeing a vision' (Tobit 12: 19). On this point Thomas Aquinas agrees with the Jewish Midrash: 'The angels that appeared to Abraham only pretended to eat.' So also in the Quran, when the angels visited Abraham they did not eat.

As angels are not born and do not die or eat or sleep, it follows that angels do not marry or have offspring. This is stated explicitly by Jesus, who said that, in the world to come, when the dead are raised, they will not marry but will be 'like the angels in heaven' (Matthew 22: 30). All the Abrahamic traditions agree that the angels were created at or soon after the beginning of the world. They are not like human beings, where one generation succeeds the next.

So much of human life is related to the cycle of life and death, to the brevity of the human lifespan, to the need for food and shelter, to the vulnerability to sickness and injury. None of this applies to angels. Milton, who thought that angels did have bodies of a kind, defended the view that angels do eat and drink (and even have sex). This was part of a seemingly deliberate attempt to humanize so as to dramatize the life of the angels. It made his angels seem somewhat like the Homeric gods of ancient Greece. Nevertheless, Milton is very much an exception in the tradition. The classical account of angels, as developed from Philo through Augustine and Dionysius to Ibn Sina, Maimonides, and Thomas Aquinas, makes angels radically different from human beings. In the Middle Ages, talk about angels was frequently an indirect way of talking about human beings. We will return to this theme at the end of the book. Angels can provide a mirror to help us appreciate human life. Nevertheless, this mirror functions predominantly by way of contrast. Thinking about angels, who do not have bodies, helps us appreciate how much of human life is in fact bound up with the fact that we do have bodies.

4

Divine Messengers

Angels as Messengers

The word angel (*malach*) is simply the ordinary Hebrew word for a messenger. The same is true in Arabic and in Greek. It is the Greek word *angelos* that is the source for the English word 'angel'. In the previous chapter we saw how philosophers such as Ibn Sina, Moses Maimonides, and Thomas Aquinas were interested in what angels were made of, or what they were not made of. Thomas understood angels essentially as pure intellects, minds without bodies. This is in contrast to human beings, who are, 'as it were, common, composed of spirit and body' (Creed of Lateran IV). However, the tradition of angels does not begin with this question of what they are made of. It begins with an encounter, with the coming of angels as messengers. According to Augustine, the word 'angel' is the name not of a nature but of a role. There is no reason not to call a human being an angel if that person is acting as a messenger. The word has come to mean someone carrying a message from God, but this someone could still be a human being. The Apostle Paul said of himself, 'you did not scorn or despise me, but received me as an angel of God' (Galatians 4: 14).

One of the key moments in the story of the Abrahamic faiths is the coming of the angels to Abraham. They came as strangers and as guests, but before they left the Lord told Abraham: 'I will surely return to you in the spring, and Sarah your wife shall have a son' (Genesis 18: 10). In the Quran the angels say 'Have no fear', and they gave good news of a knowledgeable son (51: 28). The angels are talking to Abraham, but Sarah overhears, as she is surely supposed to. It is not just a message for Abraham, the father-figure who is sitting with the angels, but perhaps more so it is a message for Sarah, the childless wife who is preparing the meal. Sarah is by this time an old woman. According to the Quran, she looks at her wrinkled skin and says, 'I am a sterile old woman' (51: 29), and so, when she hears what the angels say, she laughs.

This story is ironic on a number of levels. The intended recipient of the message is hiding in the tent. She only 'over-hears' the message. On hearing the message the woman laughs, not with joy but with bitter irony, for the message seems unbelievable. Nevertheless, this laughter will take on a new meaning when the message proves to be true and the child is born. The story is playful, but it is not a cruel playful-ness. It is the playfulness that reveals good news indirectly and by hints. This playful or ironic or half-hidden way of communicating is not the exception but it is rather charac-teristic of the stories of angelic utterances. Even if the message is clear, it is often misunderstood, and, as the story unfolds, it seems that the message has to be understood gradually.

While the story is deliberately playful and domestic, the message is not only of individual significance. The birth of Isaac is not just a moment of joy for the new parents. It also marks the beginning of the story of a people, part of its founding narrative. Abraham's son is Isaac. Isaac has two sons: Jacob and Esau. Jacob has twelve sons, and each one of these is the father of one of the twelve tribes of Israel. So what seemed to be a merely personal communication, not even heard but overheard, was also an announcement of such significance that it continues to shape the world to this day. This paradoxical mixing of the personal and the universal is also typical of the scriptural stories of angels speaking. The angelic communication is always personal, to one or two people. It is not a public announcement made before crowds or officials. It sits on the boundary of the private and the public: a message given in private but with a public significance.

The same paradoxical character of an angel's message is found in the story of Moses and the burning bush. Moses sees a bush that is on fire but that is not being burnt up. The mysterious fire is in fact an angel, who speaks to Moses out of the bush. The Lord tells Moses that he has seen the suffering of the people and is sending Moses to liberate them. Moses asks what he should say to people if they ask who has sent him. The Lord replies: 'I am who I am. Say this to the people of Israel, "I AM has sent me to you"' (Exodus 3: 14). This seems to be a reply, but others have seen it as a refusal to give a reply. The reply of the angel has left theologians with more questions and arguments than if the angel had never spoken, and yet it also seems to reveal something. The message comes from the One who simply *is* and from whom all other things have come. The attempt to give this mystery a name is resisted by the angel, but indirectly, by seeming to give a name.

Passing on the Message

The paradoxical character of angelic speech is also shown by the fact that, when an angel speaks, there is often some confusion about who is speaking. After Abraham has provided the angels with food and drink, they say to him: 'Where is Sarah your wife?' Then the Lord says: 'I will surely return to you in the spring, and Sarah your wife shall have a son.' The story switches from 'they say' to 'the Lord says'. How can this be? Are we supposed to think that one of the 'men' is the Lord and the other two are angels? This does not seem right. What is more, the same switch happens in other passages when there is only one angel present.

When Moses sees the burning bush, it is said that 'the angel of the Lord appeared to Moses in a flame of fire out of the midst of a bush' (Exodus 3: 2). But as soon as he starts speaking it is 'the Lord' who speaks. The same pattern is found when an angel appears to Gideon (Judges 6: 11–14).

Some early Christian theologians saw in this alternating of voices evidence that 'the angel of the Lord' was really Jesus, who was appearing in the form of an angel. The view that some angels were Jesus, or that Jesus was an angel, is discussed later in this chapter. Some modern interpreters of the Bible have argued that the different voices are evidence of the mixing of two versions of the story, one in which an

57

angel is speaking and one in which God is speaking. However, neither the old 'Jesus-as-an-angel' theory nor the new 'multiple-versions' theory is really necessary. There is a simpler explanation.

For the ancient Hebrew people who handed down these stories orally, and for those who first wrote the stories down, the angel of God was speaking for God. That is the whole point. If the angel is speaking for God, then sometimes the story will be told as though God is speaking directly, while at other times it will be made explicit that it is the angel who is speaking.

Gabriel the Herald

In general, in the Hebrew Scriptures, when an angel speaks, the angel becomes transparent, as it were. The voice of the angel is the voice of the one who sends the angel, and the personality of the angel itself is not visible. It was only in late books such as Daniel that angels were given names. According to the book of Daniel, Gabriel is a figure 'having the appearance of a man' who explains the meaning of Daniel's vision (Daniel 8: 15–16). He comes 'in swift flight' to give Daniel knowledge and understanding (9: 21). The name Gabriel means 'mighty man of God' (from the Hebrew *Gabar*, mighty) and has the connotation of a ruler or warrior.

The Archangel Gabriel is a popular figure who pops up in several other Jewish books and in the Talmud, but his fame stems from his role in the New Testament and in the Quran.

In the New Testament Gabriel appears first in the story of Zechariah and Elizabeth. The angel gives his name, without even being asked: 'I am Gabriel, who stands in the presence of God; and I was sent to speak to you, and to bring you this good news' (Luke 1: 19). Gabriel comes to announce the birth of John the Baptist. This story has close parallels to the story of Abraham and Sarah and the birth of Isaac. Like Sarah, Elizabeth has had no children and is now an old woman. Like Abraham, Zechariah is visited by an angel who tells him that his wife will bear a son. In the Hebrew story it is Sarah who does not believe the news, whereas in the New Testament it is Zechariah who does not believe. Because of this, Zechariah is struck dumb until after the baby is born.

This story, which is remarkable enough, is immediately eclipsed by another story that is the reason why the name of Gabriel is known in every country on earth. After having spoken to Zechariah, Gabriel is sent to a young woman called Mary, to announce to her the birth of Jesus (Luke 1: 26–7).

The announcement of the birth of Jesus is the beginning of the 'good news', which is the core of Christian belief. The story shows Jesus to be the promised saviour, the Christ, who has come with a message not only for the Jewish people but for all people. While the story of Zechariah and Elizabeth is strongly reminiscent of earlier stories in the Hebrew Scriptures, the story of Mary is something new. This is also symbolized by the fact that Zechariah and Elizabeth are old, while Mary is young.

The moment when the angel comes to Mary has captured the Christian imagination and generated sermons, poetry, music, and, not least, art. It is perhaps the most frequently depicted image of an angel. Mary is typically portrayed as a young girl, eyes cast downwards, hands across her breast

Figure 9 *The Annunciation* (here by Fra Angelico) was a favourite subject for Christian artists.

slightly pointing inwards. This gesture suggests humility, as if to say, 'how can this be?', but it is not a picture of doubt but of acceptance: 'let what you have said be done to me.' While Mary seems still, the figure of Gabriel in contrast is all activity, his hands are also crossed as a gesture of respect, but there is an urgency about the way the angel leans forward as though bursting to tell the news. The scene is sometimes portrayed as occurring in an enclosed garden, which symbolizes Mary's virginity. The artist struggles to capture a mood that is at once perplexed, accepting, and joyous. For Christians this is a key moment in the history of salvation. It is the moment when Jesus was conceived in Mary's womb and the Word was made flesh.

Many Christians are not aware of how many elements of the gospel story are repeated in the Quran. Both the story of the birth of John the Baptist and the story of the birth of Jesus occur twice in the Quran (3: 38–47; 19: 2–21). Zechariah is described as an old man without children. 'The bones have turned brittle in my body, and my hair is aflame with grey,' he says (Quran 19: 4). In response to this prayer, God sends his angels, who call to Zechariah while he stands praying in the sanctuary (3: 39). Similarly, Zechariah is struck dumb as a sign, though this is not attributed to any lack of belief.

The angels then announce: 'O Mary, God gives you good news: a word from him whose name is "The Messiah, Jesus the son of Mary. He will be prominent in this life and in the hereafter, and one of those closest to me" ' (Quran 3: 45). In the second version of this story, it is just one angel who is sent to Mary in the form of a human being. This angel says: 'I am the messenger of your Lord, to grant you a pure son' (19: 19). In the Quran, as in the New Testament, it is made clear that Mary is a virgin and that Jesus is conceived by a miracle. In the Quran, the angel is not named explicitly as Gabriel, but is referred to as 'our spirit'. In a number of places (e.g. Quran 26: 193) the Quran seems to refer to Gabriel as God's spirit or as 'the honest spirit', and it is the belief of Muslims that Gabriel appeared to Mary.

From an Islamic point of view, the culmination of Gabriel's role is in revealing God's word to the prophet Muhammad. 'Anyone who opposes Gabriel should know that he has brought down this (Quran) into your heart, in accordance with God's will' (Quran 2: 97).

Gabriel thus appears explicitly in the Scriptures of Jews, Christians, and Muslims. He is the herald: the one who announces good news and reveals the hidden plans of God. The word angel means messenger, and among the angels Gabriel is the archetypal messenger. Christians from different churches and at different times have celebrated the feast of Gabriel on different days. The feast day of the annunciation, when the angel appeared to Mary, is on 25 March (nine months before Christmas!), and Gabriel was sometimes given a feast the day before (by Western Catholics) or the day after (by Eastern Orthodox). These days it is common to celebrate the archangels together on 29 September (Catholics) or 8 November (Orthodox). Gabriel is the patron saint of messengers, postal workers, and those who work in telecommunications.

Jesus as the Great Angel

In Judaism, Christianity, and Islam, angels are seen as messengers from God. This is seen in many passages in the Hebrew Scriptures, in the New Testament, in the Talmud, and in the Quran. When God has a message, he sends an angel to deliver it. However, for Christians, the greatest messenger from God is Jesus. Jesus is not only a messenger but also the message: he is the 'Word of God'. This is a very different attitude from the way Muslims regard Muhammad. He is regarded as the last and greatest of the prophets, but the focus is not on the messenger but on the message: the written word of the Quran. It is the Quran that is regarded as the word of God. This is why Muslims do not call themselves

Mohammedans. Muhammad is not the message; he is only the messenger.

According to Christian belief, the coming of the messenger is itself the good news. One of the themes in the Hebrew Scriptures is the prophecy that God will send a saviour. This is a promise repeated in several books but especially in the book of Isaiah. The saviour will be a descendant of King David and is sometimes called the Messiah (in Hebrew) or the Christ (the same word in Greek), which means the one who is anointed with oil. Christians believe that Jesus is the Christ, the one sent by God.

In the early Church, one of the ways this was expressed was to say that Jesus was an angel, or rather *the* angel, the 'great angel'. They called him an angel because, in the book of Isaiah, the saviour was described as an angel. One of the more famous passages in the book of Isaiah (9: 6) promises the birth of a son. This passage may be familiar, because it is used a lot at Christmas time.

> For to us a child is born,
> to us a son is given;
> and the government will be upon his shoulder,
> and his name will be called,
> 'Wonderful Counselor, Mighty God,
> Everlasting Father, Prince of Peace.'

When this passage was translated in the Septuagint, the Jewish translator was perhaps embarrassed about calling the saviour 'mighty God' and instead he wrote: 'For to us a child is born ... and his name will be called "Angel of Great Counsel".'

The Septuagint was very influential among Christians, and so they took this title and applied it to Jesus. Jesus was the

'Angel of Great Counsel', the great angel who came with the good news of salvation. This way of thinking about Jesus was popular among Christians in the early Church. One of the first great Christian writers, Justin Martyr (*c*.100–65), uses the title several times in his writings.

Why is it not common any more to refer to Jesus as the great angel? The problem for Christians with this language is that it might make people think that Jesus was not really human. If a human being acts as a messenger from God, we could call him or her 'an angel'. The word angel in Hebrew or in Greek means just a messenger. However, when we hear the word 'angel', we tend to think not of human messengers but of purely spiritual messengers, like the angel Gabriel.

In the early centuries of Christianity there were some people who thought that Jesus was a saviour sent by God, but they did not believe he was really a human being. They thought he only appeared to be human, but really he was like an angel. They were called docetists, because Jesus was not really human but only seemed to be (in Greek *doceo*). Mainstream Christianity rejected docetism, as it was important for Christians that Jesus was a real human being. If Jesus was not really human, then he did not really suffer or die, and the whole message of Christianity was based on a falsehood.

Another reason that Christians hesitated to call Jesus an angel was their belief that Jesus was God-incarnate. The Council of Chalcedon (451 CE) stated that Jesus was 'truly God and truly man', but an angel is neither God nor a man.

From a Christian perspective, all that is said of the role of the angels is said supremely about Jesus. He reveals God to human beings. Hence early Christians sometimes called Jesus 'the great angel'. Even in the Middle Ages there was a famous vision of Francis of Assisi (1181–1226), who saw a seraph between whose wings was the figure of Christ Cruci-fied. From that moment the wounds of Jesus, the 'stigmata', spontaneously appeared on Francis's hands and feet. This vision has inspired various representations of Jesus as a ser-aph, from Giotto to the present day. Nevertheless, the dom-inant Christian tradition has regarded depictions of Jesus as an angel as potentially misleading. An angel is neither God nor flesh and blood, whereas Christians believe that Jesus is both 'the Word of God' and 'the Word made flesh' (John 1: 14).

Ambivalence about Angels

Christians became uneasy about calling Jesus an angel. This is a particular example of a more general pattern in Judaism, Christianity, and Islam. These religions all include beliefs and stories about angels, but they also harbour some ambivalence about angels.

The message of these religions is not ultimately from angels, and it is not for angels, and it is not, centrally, about angels. If the message is believed, then it is believed to come from God. So also the message is not a message for angels. It is for human beings. It is a message from God for human beings about how to live and how to find peace with God. Angels bring the message. Angels announce the good news. But the message does not start with them or end with them. If angels became the focus, then there would be a danger either of forgetting whom the message was from or of forgetting whom it was for.

This ambivalence is seen throughout the Jewish Scriptures. For example, according to Psalm 8 (in the Septuagint), human beings were made 'a little lower than the angels'. Later, human beings will be 'crowned with glory and honour'. This seems to imply that human beings will be higher than the angels.

The New Testament is explicit in its ambivalence. In the letter to the Hebrews angels are described as 'ministering spirits' sent to serve human beings. If the world is a banquet, then angels are the servants, human beings are the guests, and God is the host. The letter goes on to state explicitly that God is concerned 'not with angels' but with the descendants of Abraham (Hebrew 2: 16), and indeed with all human beings.

As in the New Testament, so also in the Talmud, it is explicit that at least some human beings (the good ones) are ranked higher than the angels. They will enter a heaven that even angels are not allowed to enter. When the people of Israel praise God, the angels must be silent and have to wait until the end to sing their own praise. The Talmud also picks out some particular individuals: Ezekiel, who praises God first, before the angels, and also Adam. The first human being is not only served by angels (with roast meat!) but is worshipped by them as the image of God. The idea that the angels worshipped Adam is present also in the Quran. 'And surely, we created you and then gave you shape, then we told the angels, "Prostrate to Adam", and they prostrated' (7: 11–12).

The idea that human beings should worship angels is strongly rejected in Judaism, Christianity, and Islam. In his letter to the Colossians, Paul criticizes those who insist on 'self-abasement and worship of angels' (Colossians 2: 18). Worshipping angels is self-abasing, because angels are sent to serve human beings and not to be worshipped by human beings. Similarly, the Talmud regards angel worship as a kind of idolatry. Two examples singled out are worshipping images of the cherubim and invoking the name of Michael the archangel. The Talmud is clear that no angel, however exalted, is to be worshipped as a god.

In the Hebrew Scriptures, when the angel of the Lord visits Manoah, he offers the angel a kid. The angel directs him instead to worship God. 'If you detain me, I will not eat of your food; but if you make ready a burnt offering, then offer it to the Lord' (Judges 13: 16). The same idea is even more explicit in the New Testament when John falls down to worship at the feet of the angel who has shown him the vision. The angel says to him: 'You must not do that! I am a fellow servant with you and your brothers the prophets, and with those who keep the words of this book. Worship God!' (Revelation 22: 8–9).

Commenting on passages such as these, Augustine of Hippo states that good angels are not pleased to receive worship that is due to God. This view is quoted with approval by Thomas Aquinas. During the Reformation, Protestant Christians criticized the Roman Catholic practice of making images of saints and angels. They considered this to be too close to idolatry. However, Catholics themselves are clear that it is always wrong to worship angels or to give them the honour that belongs to God alone. Worshipping angels misses the point. Angels are the messengers; they are not the message.

Close Encounters of the Angelic Kind

If even the great traditions of religious faith are ambivalent about angels, there is still more ambivalence about angels in the contemporary world. Images of angels are all around and are immediately recognizable, but people are uneasy about taking them seriously. Angels are too colourful, too quixotic, too charming to be talked of in a serious way. It is still possible, in the modern world, to say that there is a mystery behind the universe, a reason why we are here. It is relatively common to believe, or at least half-believe, that a spiritual part of the person lives on after death. Philosophers can and do talk seriously about the existence of God and the immortality of the soul. However, very few philosophers talk seriously about angels. Such discussions belong in a monastery, or in a nursery. Those who say they have actually seen angels or heard angelic voices will find a sceptical hearing. The most common reaction is likely to be that they are delusional and may be in need of medical or psychiatric help.

It is interesting that, despite this massive cultural reluctance to take angels seriously, to countenance the existence of angels as actual living beings, there are still many people who report having encountered an angel. The scholar Emma Heathcote-James has produced an interesting study of people from the United Kingdom who report having seen an angel.

She divided their experiences into sight, hearing, touch, and smell (relatively common) and looked at the context of the experience and what it had meant to the person. Perhaps surprisingly there were a great range of people who said they had encountered an angel. The majority were Christian, reflecting the population of the United Kingdom, but those who came forward also included Muslims and Jews. Thirty per cent gave no religion and, perhaps most surprisingly, 10 per cent of those who said they had experienced the presence of an angel described themselves as atheist or agnostic.

These experiences had occurred at different times in people's lives but mostly in middle age. One common feature of the respondents was a reticence to speak about it. The encounter was thought of as highly personal, but also as something that other people might misconstrue. Since writing this book I have come across a number of people who have mentioned to me that they have seen or heard an angel. Unlike Heathcote-James I have not gone out of my way to ask people about this, but when I mentioned that I was writing a book on angels people sometimes responded with their own experiences.

The kinds of experiences that Heathcote-James has highlighted should be distinguished from religious groups that focus on 'signs and wonders', on prophetic words and miracles of healing, for in that very intense atmosphere it would seem almost natural to see an angel. They should also be distinguished from post-Christian 'new-age' spiritualities in which angel guides or healing angels have a central role. There are subcultures in the modern world within which talk of angels and demons is taken very seriously.

Heathcote-James's work is interesting. It shows that, outside these subcultures, among ordinary respectable people in the modern world, whether religious or non-religious, there are people who believe that they have encountered an angel. Generally this has happened when they were alone or with one or two other people, often not in a religious setting but in some circumstance of need.

In England such people are cautious about talking about their experiences in public. Even when I was writing this book, more than one person suggested that I skip this rather odd and embarrassing phenomenon of seeing angels and concentrate instead on angels in art and in religious doctrine. However, it needs to be remembered that the art, and the religion that it expresses, has, at its roots, the experience of people who believed they were in the presence of angels, from Ezekiel to William Blake. There are no doubt some people for whom voices or visions of angels are a symptom of a mental health condition, and others for whom they are the product of some emotional disturbance or an overworked imagination. However, Heathcote-James's study showed that, for the most part, those who report having encountered angels are indistinguishable from the general population. They are unremarkable people who have experienced something remarkable. The history of reflection on angels begins as reflection on such encounters, starting with that archetypal encounter between Abraham and the strangers who visit him at Mamre.

5

Ministering Spirits

Raphael the Healer

The story of the Archangel Raphael is told in the book of Tobit. The book tells the story of a man called Tobit who is an Israelite of the tribe of Naphtali, but who lives in exile. He is an upright man and risks his life to give a proper burial to bodies of Israelites who have been killed. One evening, because it is so hot, he sleeps outside with his face uncovered and is blinded by sparrows' droppings falling into his eyes. 'I went to the physicians to be healed but the more they treated me with ointments the more my vision was obscured by the white films, until I became completely blind' (Tobit 2: 10). Meanwhile, in a town some distance away, a relative called Sarah is afflicted by a demon. She had 'been married to seven husbands, and the wicked demon Asmodeus had killed each of them before they had been with her' (Tobit 3: 8).

Tobit and Sarah both pray, and God sends an angel to help them. Tobit's son Tobias sets off, as he thinks, to collect some money from a distant relative, but he is destined to meet Sarah and fall in love and marry her. The angel Raphael accompanies Tobias in the guise of a fellow traveller. Tobias's dog also comes along. On the way they catch an enormous fish. Later Raphael uses the liver and heart of the fish as incense to drive the demon away and the gall of the fish as ointment to heal Tobit's blindness. 'And Raphael was sent to heal both of them: Tobit, by removing the white films from his eyes, so that he might see God's light with his eyes; and Sarah the daughter of Raguel, by giving her in marriage to Tobias the son of Tobit, and by setting her free from the wicked demon Asmodeus' (Tobit 3: 17). The name Raphael means 'God heals'.

It is easy to see why this tale was not included in some Bibles. Though it has a historical setting, it is really a romance. It has more in common with the colourful folklore of the Arabic *Book of One Thousand and One Nights* than with the much more restrained biblical encounter between Abraham and the angels. Nevertheless, in spite of this, or perhaps because of this, this book has remained popular and was included in the Septuagint translation of the Bible. It finds a place in Roman Catholic, Greek, and Slavonic Bibles and in the appendix to some Protestant Bibles (the part called the 'apocrypha'). The prayer of Tobias and Sarah before they get married is still a common reading at Catholic wedding ceremonies. The book of Tobit is only a dozen pages or so and is full of charming detail. It is a book of the Bible that does not take itself very seriously and is well worth a read.

The image of Raphael and Tobias has been a popular one among artists. Typically Raphael is shown with wings and a halo, next to him is a short and youthful Tobias, who is carrying the fish. Running next to them is a small dog, not a hunting dog but obviously a pet. The three figures are on a

Figure 10 *Raphael accompanying Tobias and his dog is here flanked by the archangels Michael (with sword) and Gabriel (with lily).*

journey with a purpose, but a purpose of which Tobias is as yet unaware. It is an image of pilgrimage, of life as a journey, and an image of providence or protection. These themes retain their appeal, and the story has been retold in Salley Vickers's engaging novel *Miss Garnet's Angel*, which interweaves the ancient romance with a modern fable set in Venice.

Within Orthodox Judaism, the book of Tobit is not regarded as sacred Scripture. However, the angel Raphael is named in the Talmud, together with Gabriel and Michael, as one of the angels who came to visit Abraham. Raphael is popular in the Jewish tradition as an angel of healing and was sometimes named on protective amulets, themselves associated with healing and with magic. For most of Jewish history such amulets were a common feature of Judaism, and Jewish amulets were also used by Christians. However, contemporary Judaism follows the more sober opinion of Moses Maimonides that amulets are a form of superstition and have neither religious nor medical value.

Raphael (Israfil) is also known in Islam. The name does not occur in the Quran itself but occurs in a Hadith. In Islam, Israfil is not associated with healing but is the angel who will blow his horn to signal the end of the world and the day of judgement. This is quite close to the role that Christianity gives to the Archangel Michael.

The feast of Raphael is celebrated together with that of Michael and the other angels on 29 September among Catholics and Anglicans and on 8 November among Eastern Orthodox Christians. Raphael is patron of the sick, especially those with eye problems or mental illness (those 'plagued by demons'), and is patron of those who heal the sick, especially pharmacists and apothecaries. He is also patron of lovers and of happy meetings. Raphael is the angel most associated with serendipity.

Guardian Angels

According to the story, Raphael is sent to Tobias and Sarah, not so much to give a message but to act as helper, guide, and healer. By the time of Jesus, Jews had come to believe that every human being was given into the care of his or her own guardian angel. This belief may be influenced by Zoroastrianism, which the Jews encountered in Babylon, but it is also influenced by the example of Raphael and by the verse 'he will give his angels charge of you to guard you in all your ways' (Psalm 91: 11).

For Christians, belief in guardian angels draws directly on the words of Jesus: 'See that you do not despise one of these little ones; for I tell you that in heaven their angels always behold the face of my Father who is in heaven' (Matthew 18: 10). There is an echo here of the description of Raphael as an angel who enters before the glory of the Lord (Tobit 12: 15) and Gabriel who stands in the presence of God (Luke 1: 19). It is not absolutely clear from the words of Jesus that each person has one particular angel, but this is how the saying is most commonly interpreted.

The idea of guardian angels has an enduring appeal, because it makes particular the more general doctrine of angels and makes personal the more general doctrine of providence. Someone might believe that there is an unseen world in heaven, but might not think that it impinges on earthly events. Nor is it easy to believe that the Creator of the entire cosmos would be concerned for the short and seemingly insignificant life of each person. The idea that God designates one particular angel to guard each person is a way of tying the unseen world close to the small concerns of ordinary life. Guardian angels are, as it were, small angels, angels low enough down the hierarchy to be given the task of looking after one particular person.

In the Quran it is stated that 'two recording (angels), at right and at left, are constantly recording' (50: 17). It seems that one of these records good deeds and the other records evil deeds. We should notice that the 'recording angel' in Islam is a little different from the guardian angel of Judaism and Christianity. The role of a guardian angel is to guard, to help, and hence to intervene. In contrast, the recording angel does not intervene but stands back and acts as a witness to everything that a person does, for good or for ill.

Angels at the Beginning of Life

When the three angels visit Abraham, they inform him that, by the time they return next year, Sarah will have given birth to a child, Isaac (Genesis 18: 10; Quran 51: 28). Other births that are announced by angels include those of Ishmael (Genesis 16: 11), Samson (Judges 13: 3), John the Baptist (Luke 1: 13; Quran 3: 39), and, of course, Jesus (Luke 1: 26–31; Quran 3: 45).

These stories of angels announcing a forthcoming birth may have helped give rise to the idea that angels are involved in the conception of every child. This idea can be found in each of the Abrahamic faiths. The Talmud contains a story that every soul that will ever be born was created in the first six days of creation and waits in a heaven called Arabot. 'At the time of conception God commands the angel who is the guardian of the spirits, saying, "Bring me such and such a spirit which is in paradise."'

The early Christian writer Clement of Alexandria tells a similar story. He says that the soul is first cleansed in preparation for conception and is then 'introduced by one of the angels that preside over generation'. Clement explicitly links this idea to the biblical stories of angels appearing to announce the birth of a child.

Islam also makes a link between the origin of each soul and the angels. There is a well-known saying of the prophet that describes the stages of embryonic development. In this case the angel is not present as an agent introducing the soul. The angel is present as a witness. This reflects what has already been said about guardian angels in Islam. Their role is not to intervene, but they are present, keeping a record from the beginning.

The constituents of one of you are collected for forty days in his mother's womb; it becomes something that clings in that period, then it becomes a chewed lump of flesh in the same period. And the angel is sent to him with instructions concerning four things, so the angel writes down his provision, his death, his deeds, and whether he will be wretched or fortunate. Then the soul is breathed into him.

The Jewish Midrash and the early Christian theologian seem to suggest that the soul is introduced by the angel at conception, for this is when the angels announce the forthcoming birth. In contrast, in Islam the soul is given after the body has been formed, at or sometime after forty days. There is no general agreement between religions as to precisely when the soul is given, and many contemporary Jews and Christians regard this as a mystery that God has not revealed. This reflects the view of at least one biblical writer: 'Just as you do not know when the spirit enters the bones in the mother's womb so you do not know the work of God, who makes everything' (Ecclesiastes 11: 5). There is no universal agreement as to precisely when the soul is given, but there is agreement that it is given by God through the ministry of angels.

Does this imply that each person has a guardian angel even when he or she is in the womb? According to Thomas Aquinas, an angel is appointed as guardian to each person as soon as he or she is born. This was the opinion of Jerome (c.347–420), the ancient Christian writer who translated the Bible into Latin. Thomas Aquinas saw no reason to reject this belief. Aquinas acknowledged that the child in the mother's womb already possessed a soul, but he thought that the child was so intimately bound to the mother that there was no need for a separate guardian. 'And therefore it can be said with some degree of probability that the angel who guards the mother guards the child while in the womb.' When the child is born, then an angel is appointed as his or her unique guardian.

Angels at the End of Life

As angels are particularly associated with the coming-to-be of new life, they are also associated with the end of life. The most common place to find statues or images of angels is at a graveyard. When someone dies, he or she goes to be with the angels. Jesus said in one of his parables that when the poor man Lazarus died he was 'carried by the angels to Abraham's bosom' (Luke 16: 22).

There is a common view that when human beings die they become angels. However, in orthodox Judaism, Christianity,

Figure 11 Angels are a familiar sight in Christian cemeteries.

and Islam, angels are not the souls of dead people. Angels are a different kind of creature altogether. Angels are not born and do not die. They do not live the fleeting transient life of human beings. They stand more above time than in time. Nevertheless, there is clearly something in common between human beings and angels, and especially between good human beings who have died and good angels who are in heaven. Jesus himself says that, in the resurrection, people 'cannot die anymore, because they are like angels' (Luke 20: 36).

It was common, especially in Victorian times, to think that children who die become angels. This is because of their lack of experience of the world and their innocence. All adults have done some things they regret (or that they should regret), but young children have not yet made mistakes in life. It is almost as though they die before they have lived. This is why they are like the angels who have never experienced the human world of time and change. The theologian Simon Tugwell has called this 'glorified inexperience'.

For adults death brings judgement. This view is shared by all the Abrahamic faiths and has echoes in philosophers as diverse as Plato and Heidegger (1889–1976). When someone dies, his or her life comes to an end, and the person can be judged for what he or she has done with this life. This darker aspect of death, death as judgement, calls for a darker angel, an angel of death.

In the Bible the angel of the Lord sometimes comes as an angel of death, on one occasion killing 185,000 Assyrian soldiers (2 Kings 19: 35). In the book of Revelation there are angels with sharp sickles who go into the world to reap the harvest, and to gather wicked souls into the great wine press of God's anger (Revelation 14: 19–20). Though the book describes more than one angel with a sickle, it is this imagery that has given us the picture of 'the grim reaper', an angel who is the very personification of death.

The image of the grim reaper is associated in particular with the time of the Black Death, the worst pandemic in recorded history, which wiped out perhaps half the entire European population. No one was safe from an early and painful death. Nevertheless, people continued to make human and religious sense of death. They saw death as a moment of judgement and as the great leveller. This context gave rise to the common medieval image of the 'dance of death', which everyone is forced to join, whether they are a Lord or a serf, a bishop or a housewife. Life finds its measure and its meaning in death. The same theme using the same imagery is explored in the classic Ingmar Bergman film *The Seventh Seal*, in which a knight plays chess with the grim reaper. To find God the knight must first face death.

The imagery of the grim reaper and the last judgement is a response to the experience of great communal suffering, of plague, war, or persecution. This is obviously true of the medieval imagination after the Black Death. It is equally true of the imagery of the book of Revelation, and of earlier Jewish books such as Daniel and Enoch. These books were written at a time of terrible persecution. They use violent images to make sense of violent times. Nevertheless, death often comes gently or after a long life, and the association of angels with death is more often to bring comfort to death than to emphasize its terror. The angels who carry the poor man to paradise in Jesus's parable (Luke 16: 22) are surely consoling angels. In Islamic tradition (but not in the Quran) there is an angel of death, Malak al-Maut (sometimes called Azrael), who separates the soul from the body. The sight of this angel is pleasant for believers but is terrifying for the wicked.

A consoling angel is portrayed in the poem of John Henry Newman *The Dream of Gerontius*, which was set to music by Edward Elgar. When Gerontius is on the point of death, he meets an angel who sings:

> My Father gave in charge to me
> This child of earth
> E'en from its birth,
> To serve and save,
> Alleluia,
> And saved is he

The angel who has cared for Gerontius throughout life as his guardian angel now has the task of greeting him and taking him 'home' from earth to heaven. The angel who accompanies invisibly in life appears at the moment of death. In this way the figure of the guardian angel links the believer's trust in God's providence throughout life with his or her hope in God's mercy beyond death.

Entertaining Angels Unawares

Many stories of angelic encounters, both in folklore and in a popular culture, associate angels with help, protection, or rescue. The contemporary phenomenon of these kinds of encounters was discussed at the close of the previous chapter. In these encounters, when angels appear in the guise of a stranger, it is most frequently to offer some practical help— for example, to give directions to someone who is lost. However, within the Abrahamic tradition there are also stories in which angels appear not as helpers but as strangers in need of help.

The great biblical example of this is again the story of Abraham and the three young men. They come to him as strangers and he shows them hospitality. It is this story that the New Testament writer has in mind when he urges Christians: 'Do not neglect to show hospitality to strangers, for thereby some have entertained angels unawares' (Hebrews 13: 2).

This New Testament quotation was used for the title of the 1996 film with Moira Kelly and Martin Sheen *Entertaining Angels: The Dorothy Day Story*. Dorothy Day (1897–1980) was a journalist and peace activist. She was both an anarchist and a convert to Roman Catholicism. In 1927 Dorothy Day, together with Peter Maurin (1877–1949), founded the Catholic Worker Movement, which established houses of hospitality to work with and for the poor. This began in New York City and now has houses throughout the world.

The theme of showing hospitality to angels develops in a particular way within the Christian tradition. This can be seen, for example, in the story of Martin of Tours (316–97), a Roman soldier who lived in the fourth century CE. Martin encountered a naked beggar in winter time. Having no extra clothes to give to the beggar, Martin took his sword and cut his own cloak in half, giving half to the beggar. The following night Martin had a dream in which Jesus appeared wearing the robe. Jesus said to the angels who were around him: 'Martin, who is not yet baptised, has clothed me with this robe.' Subsequently Martin left the army and became a monk. Later, and with some reluctance, he became Bishop of Tours. In a Christian context the idea of showing hospitality is linked not only to angels but directly to Jesus, who said 'as you did it to one of the least of these my brethren, you did it to me' (Matthew 25: 40).

It is also significant that the story of Martin of Tours concerns not simply a stranger but a poor man. This represents a particular Christian emphasis. Nevertheless, the idea at root is the same. Both Martin's clothing of the beggar and Dorothy Day's social activism build directly on the ancient virtue of hospitality to strangers of the kind shown by Abraham to the angels.

6

Heavenly Hosts

Jacob's Ladder

And Jacob came to a certain place, and stayed there that night, because the sun had set. Taking one of the stones of the place, he put it under his head and lay down in that place to sleep. And he dreamed that there was a ladder set up on the earth, and the top of it reached to heaven; and behold, the angels of God were ascending and descending on it!

Then Jacob awoke from his sleep and said, 'Surely the Lord is in this place; and I did not know it.' And he was afraid, and said, 'How awesome is this place! This is none other than the house of God, and this is the gate of heaven.'   (Genesis 28: 11–12, 16–17)

The starting point for this book has been the story about Abraham being visited by angels. The account of Jacob's dream occurs in the same cycle of stories. Jacob is the son of Isaac, the grandson of Abraham. However, unlike the encounter between Abraham and the angels, the story of Jacob's dream does not occur in the Quran; hence the image of Jacob's ladder is confined to Judaism, Christianity, and to Western culture.

It is significant that Jacob's vision of a ladder between heaven and earth occurs in a dream. The ladder can be understood as a metaphor for the spiritual world 'above'.

Figure 12 William Blake's portrayal of Jacob's ladder.

As argued earlier, angels do not have bodies and so they cannot exist in a place either above or below the earth. The imagery of ascending and descending is figurative rather than literal. There cannot be a physical ladder between two worlds, but the ladder is a depiction of the relationship between the physical and the spiritual realm. The place where Jacob rests when he has this dream he calls the gate of heaven because there he glimpses a world that is 'other' or holy, a world beyond this world.

Jacob sees angels ascending and descending, not human beings. Nevertheless, as was seen in the previous chapter in relation to Raphael, angels are commonly depicted as companions to human beings on their journey. Thus the image of angels ascending and descending naturally suggests that human beings might ascend on this same ladder. This idea is taken a step further by Philo, who saw in this text a reflection of the philosophy of Plato. According to Philo, human souls first existed separately from the body, and, because they lost their purity of vision, they 'fell' into bodies. At death there is an opportunity to escape from the body, but those who are weighed down by material concerns and physical desires will quickly return to the body.

The sky is like a populous city, it is full of imperishable and immortal citizens, souls equal in number to the stars. Now of these souls some descend upon the earth with a view to being bound up in mortal bodies, those namely which are most nearly connected with the earth, and which are lovers of the body. But some soar upwards, being again distinguished [from the body] ... Of these, those which are influenced by a desire for mortal life, and which have been familiarised to it, again return to it.

Both mainstream Judaism and mainstream Christianity came to reject the idea of souls falling into bodies and later rising to heaven. The belief that human beings might have many reincarnations in different bodies has no basis in the Jewish Scriptures. This belief also takes away from the significance of this one life and from the seriousness of judgement that comes with death. According to mainstream Jewish, Christian, and indeed also Islamic theology, the person is judged after death once and for all. Life is not a game in which the player gets a second go.

Jews and Christians have not generally understood ascending and descending on Jacob's ladder in terms of reincarnation. However, this image has commonly been used for the human spiritual journey. Life can be understood as a journey upwards in search of 'higher' things, a journey towards God, accompanied by the angels. In the New Testament Jesus tells Nathaniel, 'you will see heaven opened, and the angels of God ascending and descending upon the Son of Man' (John 1: 51). Here Jesus identifies himself ('the Son of Man') as the stairway between heaven and earth. On this basis many Christian writers from Augustine to the Methodist John Wesley (1703–91) have identified Jacob's ladder with Jesus, or sometimes with the cross of Jesus.

The idea of a ladder to perfection is used in the Benedictine Rule, one of the first written rules for Christian monks. It also provides the title for one of the most popular spiritual works of the Middle Ages: *The Scale of Perfection* by Walter Hilton (1340–96). In Dante's *Divine Comedy* St Benedict complains that no one will lift a foot to climb Jacob's ladder any more— because the Church has grown greedy and self-indulgent.

The idea of a ladder to perfection also lies behind the popular children's game 'snakes and ladders'. However, this game originates not from the Judaeo-Christian tradition but from a similar Hindu idea of a ladder of salvation. The game was introduced to Britain from India in the nineteenth century.

In literature, the image of Jacob's ladder has been invoked by poets such as John Dryden (1631–1700) to symbolize the progress of the human spirit: 'Where ev'ry age do's on another move.' This idea is turned to romantic love in Thomas Carlyle (1795–1881), who writes of women 'in whose hand [is] the invisible Jacob's ladder, whereby man might mount into very heaven'.

The 1946 British film with David Niven *A Matter of Life and Death* was released in the United States as *A Stairway to Heaven*. It ends with a scene of the heavenly stairway as an escalator (used on the cover of Phil Collins's single 'Something Happened on the Way to Heaven'). There are some parallels here to the profound but disturbing 1990 film with Tim Robbins, *Jacob's Ladder*. This concerns a man who is given an experimental drug in Vietnam and is subsequently afflicted by demons. The theme of the film is that his torment need not be a hopeless hell but can be a hopeful purgatory—a painful ascent towards release from earthly attachments. In the film Jacob is helped by his chiropractor played by Danny Aiello, who is his guardian angel.

There is no evidence of direct influence of Jacob's ladder on the Led Zeppelin song 'Stairway to Heaven', but perhaps there is an unconscious influence. In the song the stairway to heaven is an ironic reference to happiness that can be bought for gold. The ironic usage relies on the idea that there is a happiness that cannot be bought. This is the true stairway to heaven.

Angels or Aliens?

In the 1970s the alien enthusiast Eric Von Däniken (1935–) caused a controversy by claiming that Abraham and Jacob did not meet angels but aliens. They received not supernatural visitors but extraterrestrial visitors. This claim was part of an ambitious project to see evidence in archaeology and ancient texts for previous visits to earth by extraterrestrials. One of Von Däniken's favourite examples was the vision of Ezekiel of the four living creatures and the 'a wheel within a wheel' on the rims of which are 'many eyes' (Ezekiel 1: 4–28) According to Von Däniken, this passage describes an encounter between Ezekiel and alien visitors. Von Däniken even worked with a NASA engineer, Josef Blumrich, to produce a design for a spacecraft based on the Ezekiel account.

The passage from Ezekiel contains many strange and powerful images. It is easy to see how a modern reader, unfamiliar with the original context, would struggle to make sense of these images, or even see them as a description of an alien spaceship. What was the original context? The book of Ezekiel was written at a time when the kingdom of Judah had been defeated by the Babylonian army and many Jews had been taken into captivity. One of the most traumatic aspects of that defeat was the desecration of the Temple. This holy place built by Solomon and the centre of Jewish worship for centuries was destroyed by a foreign army. The whole book of Ezekiel is shaped by imagery taken from the Temple in Jerusalem, and it contains a promise that the Temple will be rebuilt and will be the centre of a renewed Israel.

The passage about the four living creatures uses especially the imagery of the cherubim, statues of which had stood in the sanctuary before the Temple was desecrated. It also evokes the cloud of glory that covered Mount Sinai when Moses received the Ten Commandments (Exodus 19: 16). This was already associated with the Temple (Exodus 40: 34; Levitus 16: 2). The language of the book of Ezekiel thus makes sense in relation to the message he was communicating about the Temple, its destruction, and the glory of God. Ezekiel uses awesome images to emphasize the mysterious power of God. This imagery evokes what Rudolf Otto (1869–1937) called the experience of the 'numinous'.

The earth-shattering events that shape the book of Ezekiel are not alien visitations but the religious and political catastrophe of defeat at the hands of the Babylonians. There is simply no need to postulate flying saucers in order to understand this ancient text. Like many of Von Däniken's examples from archaeology and ancient religious writings, he neglects the original context and reads something into the text for which there is no evidence.

What is it though that drives people to find aliens in ancient religious documents? In the Middle Ages there was a common word view held by Jews, Christians, and Muslims that combined elements of Aristotle's philosophy with a theology taken from the sacred Scriptures. The world was understood as a coherent cosmos in which angelic forces moved the stars and the planets. This harmony was the 'song of the spheres', and human beings had a meaningful place within it. In the seventeenth century, when the physics of Descartes and Newton replaced the physics of Aristotle, it seemed to many that this music of the spheres had been silenced. Hence the haunting words of Pascal: 'the eternal silence of these infinite spaces fills me with dread.' After Newton the world was not a meaningful cosmos but a silent empty space infinite in all directions.

Modern physics has brought back a sense of a finite and interelated cosmos, but it is still without the angels who once gave voice to this cosmic harmony. Bryan Appleyard in *Aliens: Why They Are Here* argues that fascination with aliens is, at least in part, an expression of nostalgia for angels—that is to say, for an earth that lies at the base of Jacob's ladder. Rather than seeing ancient religious texts as evidence for alien visitors, we should perhaps see modern interest in aliens as the metamorphosis of an ancient belief. This is why interest in aliens is often so personal and why it remains strong in modern Western culture, despite the dearth of good scientific evidence. The possibility of extraterrestrial visitors functions less as a scientific hypothesis and more as a form of quasi-religious belief. Aliens are angels for modern materialists. It is ironic that contemporary belief in aliens gives rise to a peculiarly literalistic reading of ancient texts, as though Jacob's ladder was reduced to the stepladder hanging down from a space ship. In contrast, a religious belief in angels challenges the view that the world can be understood purely in physical terms. Jacob's ladder invites a spiritual rather than a phyiscal journey.

Celestial Hierarchies

The word hierarchy means sacred rule or order. It is accidental, though perhaps helpful when talking of angels, that in English it sounds a little like 'higher'-archy. This reinforces the image of higher, middle, and lower ranks. In the army, for example, there is a 'chain of command' from top to bottom and a chain of information from bottom to top. In the world view of medieval theologians, both Jewish and Christian, the hierarchy of angels is part of the 'chain of being' linking all creatures in one ordered cosmos from top (God) to bottom (inert matter).

It would be fair to say that modern society is ambivalent about the idea of hierarchy. Hierarchical structures remain in society, especially in big companies, in corporations, and in government, but people are also aware that hierarchy can be a form of political oppression. This is so because human beings are essentially equal by nature. Distinctions between people should be only for certain purposes and when and if these distinctions are helpful for the common good. Human hierarchies need to be challenged when they have become corrupt or tyrannical. In contrast, the hierarchy of angels is essential to them and is reliably benign, being related to the good purposes of God. By nature human beings are placed 'lower than the angels', but the message of Christianity is that human beings can 'ascend' higher if they grow in faith, hope, and love. The image of Jacob's ladder is not of a fixed hierarchy but of constant movement up and down. In the Christian tradition this image is generally applied to the whole human race—it is a ladder that all are invited to climb.

The idea of an ordered set of different ranks of angels provides a place for the different kinds of angels mentioned in the Scriptures—and particularly for cherubim and seraphim—and it also provides a rationale to distinguish angels and archangels. It is around the time of Jesus that we have the first systematic listing of the heavenly hierarchy. The book of Enoch mentions seven ranks of angels: cherubim, seraphim, ofanim (wheels, from the vision of Ezekiel), angels of power, principalities, the messiah, and the elemental powers (Enoch 61:10 ff.) The seven ranks of angels echo the seven archangels listed in Enoch and referred to in Tobit. The number seven also relates to the seven days of creation and the law of the Sabbath. It is a sacred number within Judaism. The Testament of Levi has a slightly different list but still describes seven ranks of angels and also describes seven heavens.

Things get a bit more complicated with the Slavonic version of the book of Enoch, which has seven heavens but also has ten ranks of angels. Ten is a sacred number in Judaism because of the Ten Commandments. Within the Talmud and in later Rabbinic Judaism this combination of seven heavens and ten ranks of angels becomes dominant. The seven heavens as listed in the Talmud are: velon, rakia, shehakim, zebul, maon, makon, and arabot. There are several lists of the ten ranks of angels but perhaps the most influential is that of Moses Maimonides: hayyot, ofanim, arelim, hashmallim, seraphim, angels (malakim), gods (elohim), sons of God (bene Elohim), cherubim, and men (ishim). Thus, faced with a choice of two sacred numbers, Judaism has chosen both and has ten ranks of angels as well as seven heavens. Unfortunately this leaves the believer somewhat confused.

There is no agreed or simple scheme that shows how the ten ranks of angels relate to the seven heavens or to the seven archangels.

The idea of a heavenly hierarchy was popular in first-century Judaism, and this shaped the view found in the New Testament. In one of his letters Paul writes that he was 'caught up to the third heaven' (2 Corinthians 12: 2). Paul also speaks of angels, principalities, and powers (Romans 8: 38), or, again, of principalities and powers in the heavenly places (Ephesians 3: 10; see also 6: 12). In another letter Paul writes of thrones, dominions, principalities, or authorities (Colossians 1: 16). Similarly Peter in his letter writes that Jesus 'has gone into heaven and is at the right hand of God, with angels, authorities, and powers subject to him' (1 Peter 3: 22). All these terms—thrones, dominions, principalities, authorities, and powers—occurred in the Jewish literature of the time and were common to Christians and Jews. There was a shared view that there were ranks of angels, but in the New Testament it is not clear how many ranks of angels there are supposed to be or how many heavens or what their names are.

Within Christianity the most influential writer on angelic hierarchies came much later. He was a fifth-century monk, but he wrote under the name Dionysius the Areopagite, the convert from Athens mentioned in the New Testament (Acts 17: 34). Dionysius was strongly influenced by the philosophy of Neoplatonism, and his approach to writing about God and angels has been called 'mystical'.

Both in Neoplatonism and in Christianity the most sacred number is three. This is the number of the Trinity, of the Christian God who is three-in-one, Father, Son, and Holy

Spirit. The Neoplatonic philosopher Plotinus (*c*.204–70) had also developed a trinity, the One, Intellect (*nous*), Soul (*psyche*), from which the rest of the world comes forth. Dionysius therefore described not seven or ten ranks of angels but three-times-three ranks: three hierarchies of angels each containing three orders. He took the names of the resulting nine ranks of angels by combining the terms and lists given in the Old and New Testaments. The resulting scheme was as follows:

First hierarchy: seraphim, cherubim, thrones
Second hierarchy: dominions, virtues, powers
Third hierarchy: principalities, archangels, angels.

In the understanding of Dionysius and of Thomas Aquinas, Dante, Milton, and those many writers who followed Dionysius, the three hierarchies have different functions. The first hierarchy is unconcerned with worldly matters and is completely absorbed in love of God. The highest order in this hierarchy is the seraphim. Their name comes from the Hebrew *sarap* meaning fire and is taken to refer to the fire of the love of God. Like the cherubim, the seraphim are associated with the throne of God:

I saw the Lord sitting upon a throne, high and lifted up; and his train filled the Temple. Above him stood the seraphim; each had six wings: with two he covered his face, and with two he covered his feet, and with two he flew. And one called to another and said: 'Holy, holy, holy is the LORD of hosts; the whole earth is full of his glory.'

(Isaiah 6: 1–3; see also Revelation 4: 8)

The second hierarchy is concerned with the government of the world and of nations. Hence the names of the orders in this hierarchy are terms for government: dominions, virtues, powers. The third and lowest order of angels is the one most concerned with particular earthly matters. It is here we find the guardian angels and the angels that appear to people.

The scheme of three hierarchies with different functions works reasonably for the first and third hierarchies. They are fairly clear what their roles are. It works less well for the middle ranks of angels. Even Dionysius, who had something to say about all the angels, was less convincing when he tried to explain the difference between dominions, virtues, powers, and principalities. It is hardly surprising that Gregory the Great (c.540–604) put these middle ranks in a slightly different order (Thomas Aquinas, Dante, and Milton follow Dionysius rather than Gregory).

We should spare a thought for the middle management of the angelic world, too far above human concerns to be guardians and messengers, too far from the throne to be concerned only with heavenly things. The significance of these distinct orders, from a human perspective, is only to illuminate the general point that there is a great diversity of angels and that there is a place for each within the whole. Thomas Aquinas argues that not only each order or angels but every single angel has its own role and office, but that human knowledge of angels, even with the help of the Scriptures, is very imperfect and allows us to make distinctions in only a general way.

According to the Christian tradition, the role of the angels is thus twofold at root: they are archetypal adorers of God and they are messengers or interveners. While the idea of different functions of different ranks of angels might lead to angelic specialization, this can be true only up to a point. All the angels worship God in heaven and all are concerned that

God's purposes on earth are fulfilled. In Christian tradition these two roles have sometimes been called the contemplative (prayer, reflection, adoration) and the active (working for others, healing, teaching).

Human beings, like angels, might also specialize. Nevertheless, the traditional doctrine of angels points to the fundamental unity of contemplative and active roles. This has social and political implications. Clearly society needs people to devote themselves to practical and pragmatic activities. Nevertheless, society also needs a sense of direction and needs to renew itself and for this it needs some people to focus on seeking truth, beauty, and human meaning for their own sake. As all angels combine contemplation and action, so equally all human beings need some space to contemplate and examine their lives if they are going to flourish in their activity.

Angels in the Liturgy

The brief history of angels sketched in Chapter 1 drew attention to the time of exile in Babylon when the Temple was central as a symbol of hope and unity for the people. This is evident in the book of Ezekiel. After the leaders of the people had returned from their exile, they rebuilt the Temple and gave it an even greater place in Jewish life than it had had before.

The revived prominence of the Temple is the context within which people start to imagine a heavenly Temple, with heavenly rituals or 'liturgy' performed by the angels. And, just as there is a hierarchy among the angels in heaven, so there is a hierarchy of who does what in the Temple rituals. There are some who, like the highest angels, are allowed to enter the sanctuary, and there are others who busy themselves with practical matters. This is obviously an idea that was attractive to priests and later to monks and nuns. It can be seen in the theology of Dionysius and it is one of the reasons for thinking that he was a monk.

The Temple was decorated with angels (cherubim), and angels were almost certainly mentioned in the Temple liturgies. Though it is not possible to piece together exactly what went on in the Temple liturgy, it seems very likely that psalms were sung and that some of the psalms were written for that purpose. The psalms as we now have them contain several references to the angels praising God—for example, 'Bless the Lord, O you his angels, you mighty ones who do his will' (Psalm 103: 20). This or psalms like this would have had a place in the ancient liturgy of the Jews. It is likely that other passages, such as the 'Holy, holy, holy' (Isaiah 6: 3), were also used liturgically.

In contemporary Jewish liturgy the angels are certainly prominent. Virtually every prayer service will include a prayer of sanctification called the *Kedusha*, at the heart of which is the recitation of holy, holy, holy: '*Kadosh, Kadosh, Kadosh.*' Many other prayers also speak of the angels praising God or bless God for creating the angels. According to the Talmud, angels visit Jewish homes at the beginning of the Sabbath, and so there is a common prayer said to welcome these angels. Either this is included in the Friday prayers at the synagogue, or in some traditions it is used at the Friday evening meal at home.

Figure 13 Jan Van Eyck's altar frontal in Ghent shows the heavenly choir singing, but without either wings or halos.

Among Christian rituals, the most central is the Eucharist, also called the Lord's Supper and 'the Mass'. This service generally includes the singing of the 'holy, holy, holy', the *sanctus* (which is Latin for 'holy'). It is introduced by words that explicitly link the church service with the activity of the angels—for example, 'And so, with all the choirs of angels in heaven, we proclaim your glory and join in their unending hymn of praise'. This not only shows a parallel in the actions of worshippers and the song of the angels in heaven and on earth; it shows further that the person who worships God is actually joining in with the angels.

The prayers of the Mass have been an inspiration and a challenge to composers through the centuries. As there is a history of the visual portrayal of angels, there is thus also a history of the music of the angels. Composers from Palestrina (1525–94), to Mozart (1756–91), to contemporary composers such as James Macmillan (1959–), have each written music for the sanctus, and each has sought to capture the voice of the angels. To take but one example, the Sanctus from Bach's (1685–1750) Mass in B Minor seeks to evoke the ranks of angels by the ascending scales, repeated musical phrases, and interweaving of parts.

In addition to classical music and liturgy, angels are ubiquitous in more popular forms of music. Just as at Christmas angels decorate shops, homes, and offices as much as they do churches, so also the sound of carols such as 'Hark! The Herald Angels Sing', 'Ding Dong Merrily on High', and 'O Come All ye Faithful' are seemingly inescapable. There are also innumerable pop songs about angels from Abba and 'I Believe in Angels' to 'Angels' by Robbie Williams. Indeed, it sometimes seems that there are few pop musicians who have not referred to angels at least in passing. These familiar tunes may not have the aspirations of high art to open the gate of heaven, but they relate the theme of heaven to the mundane and the everyday, and this also is a role of angels. It is a theme of this book that angels are as much at home in folk culture as they are in formal religious settings.

How Many Angels are There?

Dionysius has three hierarchies each with three orders of angels, but how many individual angels are there? Earlier we mentioned the argument of Thomas Aquinas that every angel is a different species. No two are alike. Does this mean that there are only nine angels? Far from it. The common view of Jews, Christians, and Muslims is that there are a great number of angels. The Jewish and Christian Scriptures give the number 'thousands of thousands and tens of thousands of tens of thousands' (Daniel 7: 10; Revelation 5: 11). If we took this literally, this would be hundreds of millions of angels, which sounds a lot, but even several hundred million would not be enough for everyone in the world to have one guardian angel each (or the two recording angels each that are mentioned in the Quran). Furthermore, against taking this literally, it should be pointed out that 'tens of thousands of tens of thousands' (myriads of myriads) is a typical way to say an uncountable number.

If every person has a guardian angel, and no angel can be a guardian to more than one person at a time, then there must be at least as many angels as people—that is, around seven billion angels. Furthermore, if guardian angels are all from the lowest order of the lowest hierarchy, and if all the orders are equally populous, this gives a figure of sixty-three billion angels. Thomas Aquinas (in the *Summa Theologiae* Ia 23.7) tells us some people say that the total number of human beings in heaven will be the same as the number of angels who fell (one-third of the total, see Revelation 12: 4). However, this could help us only if we knew how many people would be saved, which we do not. In any case, Thomas Aquinas rejects the whole idea of linking the number of angels and the number of people who will be saved. People are saved by God's mercy and by how they respond to that mercy. It is not that heaven has a limited seating capacity.

How else can we calculate how many angels there are? There is a saying attributed to the prophet Muhammad that Gabriel once revealed to him that every day 70,000 angels enter the seventh heaven for the first time. If this has been going on since the beginning of the material universe, at the modern estimate of the date for the big bang, this would give

$$70{,}000 \times 365 \text{ days} \times 14 \text{ billion years} = 350{,}000 \text{ million million angels}$$

This is an exceedingly large figure, but it is still less than the number of the stars. The number of angels has often been linked to the number of the stars. In biblical imagery the glory of the stars in the sky is often used to represent the glory of the angels and the saints in heaven. Aristotle asserted that each heavenly body was moved by an immaterial intelligence, and Moses Maimonides therefore argued that there were as many angels as heavenly bodies. Modern estimates of the number of stars in the cosmos are uncertain and tend to be revised upwards every few years. In 2003 NASA gave an estimate of seventy million million million.

Any attempt to calculate the number of angels is, of course, deliberately whimsical. The general view in Judaism, Christianity, and Islam is that the number of angels is unknown, but that it is an unimaginably large number. Rather than try to put a figure on it, Matthew Fox has suggested that we should just think that angels 'exist in astronomical numbers'. This reflects the view of Maimonides. Thomas Aquinas, following Dionysius, thinks that angels must exist in even bigger numbers than this. He argues that the number of spiritual beings incomparably exceeds all the multitude of material things, even the stars.

Related to the total number of angels is the alleged question of how many angels can dance on the head of a pin. This was supposed to be a question debated by Christian theologians in the Middle Ages. According to Isaac D'Israeli (1766–1848), the father of the British Prime Minister, Thomas Aquinas once asked: 'How many angels can dance on the point of a very fine needle, without jostling one another?' However, D'Israeli did not read Aquinas. He took this idea from a satirical writer of the seventeenth century. It goes back no further. The idea that theologians debated this question is in fact a modern invention, like the idea that people in the Middle Ages thought the world was flat (they did not—anyone with an education knew the earth was a globe). On the other hand, Thomas Aquinas did ask whether more than one angel could act at a point. This was really a way to ask about physics—how many forces can act at a point? Thomas answers that only one angel can act at a point (for comparison, a modern physicist would say that more than one force can act at a point, but that only one force results).

It might seem that the attempt to specify a number of angels makes a mockery of the existence of angels. How could there be a particular finite number of angels? However, the question should not be dismissed. If angels exist, then there is a definite number, just as there is a number of stars in the universe and a number of species of butterfly. Furthermore, even if this number cannot be known, the attempt to identify it usefully reminds us of a deeper connection between angels and number. Theoretical speculation about angels has often been connected to numbers, to threes, sevens, tens, and thousands, and this may be because numbers like angels are immaterial. Philosophers influenced by Plato have tended to have a realist account of numbers—as though numbers exist 'out there' before we learn about them: numbers are discovered not invented. Angels are not mathematical objects, but, according to this way of thinking, they do both have something in common: they are immaterial realities that impinge upon the material world.

Michael the Commander

The Archangel Michael is named in Jewish (Daniel 10: 13, 21; 12: 1), Christian (Jude 9; Revelation 12: 7), and Islamic (Quran 2: 98) scriptures and in many ancient Jewish and Christian writings. The name Michael means 'Who is like God?' and is said to be a battle cry. Certainly Michael is the most military of the named archangels. In art he is always portrayed with a sword or a lance in his hand, often in battle with the Devil (Revelation 12: 7).

In the book of Daniel, Michael is said to be a 'one of the chief princes' (10: 13) and 'the great prince who has charge of your people' (12: 1). This gives the impression that, as each individual has a guardian angel, each nation has an archangel who watches over it. In this scheme, Michael is the archangel who has care of the people of Israel. It is no surprise, then, that devotion to Michael as protector of the people has remained strong among Jews, even when Rabbis were discouraging people from invoking angels. Prayers should be directed towards God. Nevertheless, it is consoling to think that one has a supernatural champion fighting for you. Michael is even named in prayers in the Jewish liturgy.

In Islam, Michael (Mikhail) is less prominent than Gabriel (Jibril), as Gabriel has the role of speaking to Muhammad. However, in Christianity Michael is at least as popular as Gabriel. This is perhaps for two reasons. First, Michael is the archangel who drove the Devil out of heaven and so is invoked especially for protection against the Devil.

The second reason Michael remains popular is the connection between Michael and the military. Michael was the defender of the people of Israel in war. In the same way, Christian knights also invoked Michael as their protector. He is alleged to have appeared to the Emperor Constantine at his new capital of Constantinople, and to have given him military victories. In Italy in the seventh century the Lombards believed that Michael's intervention gave them a victory against the Greek Neapolitans. There are other stories

Figure 14 Joan of Arc here pictured with the Archangel Michael.

of interventions of named or unnamed angels in war. In the First World War the story spread of an angel bowman defending the British at Mons. However, in this case the appearance of the angel seems to be a rumour based ultimately on a fictional account in a newspaper.

Perhaps the most famous association of Michael and military intervention was his appearance to the young French woman Joan of Arc (1412–31). By any measure this is a remarkable story. In the early fifteenth century England had captured much of northern France, including Paris, and were poised to take the whole country. The only major town in northern France that the English did not control was Orleans. The town was not expected to hold out. In the midst of these great events an unknown girl of 12 years old had a vision in which Michael, together with two female saints, Catherine and Margaret, told her to rid France of the English.

At the age of 16, despite being an unknown young woman who was not a noble, she gained access to the French court and impressed them with a prediction of victory at Orleans. Dressed as a man, she joined the army as a standard-bearer and also gained a reputation as a skilled military strategist. For two years the French army enjoyed remarkable success, but in 1430 she was captured by the English. A group of English bishops was assembled to condemn Joan as a heretic for the offence of wearing men's clothing. She was burned at the stake in what most people at the time regarded as no more than a political execution. Joan was exonerated at a retrial immediately after the war and remained a figure of devotion in France. She was belatedly canonized by the Roman Catholic Church in 1920.

In 1886 Pope Leo XIII (1810–1903) proclaimed that all Catholics should pray to the Archangel Michael after Mass:

Saint Michael the Archangel,
Defend us in battle;
Be our protection against the wickedness and snares of the Devil.
May God rebuke him, we humbly pray:
And do thou, O Prince of the heavenly host,
By the power of God,
Thrust into hell Satan and all the evil spirits
Who prowl about the world seeking the ruin of souls.
Amen

Initially this prayer was directed to protecting the Pope's political independence; later it was directed to restoring freedom of religion in Russia. Both aims mix the themes of spiritual and temporal conflict. Since 1964 this prayer has no longer been part of the regular prayer of the Church, but it remains popular among Catholics.

Michael is typically portrayed as a warrior with sword unsheathed, but, like Raphael, he is also associated with healing. Pope Gregory the Great prayed to Michael to save Rome from the plague, and Michael appeared in a church where the sick gathered to avoid the plague. After this event the church became known as Castel Sant'Angelo. In the Eastern Orthodox Church Michael is also associated with healing. He is said to have brought forth a healing spring near Colossae. There are other springs dedicated to Michael throughout the East, and this perhaps lies behind the dedication of the Nile to his patronage.

His feast day in the West is 29 September, which was once known as Michaelmas. The word is still used for the winter term at Oxford and Cambridge universities. The principal feast day of Michael among Eastern Orthodox is 8 November. In both traditions this feast day is now a joint celebration for all the archangels. Michael is patron saint of policemen and of other emergency workers, and in Australia the National Police Remembrance Day is commemorated on 29 September.

In Jewish and Christian tradition Michael is certainly the chief of the archangels, but it is not clear how this fits with the complete celestial hierarchy. According to Dionysius' hierarchies, if Michael were top angel, this would make him a seraph, rather than an archangel. This was the view of Bonaventure (1221–74). Others put him above all the hierarchies, but this would mean he did not really belong anywhere. The whole point of the celestial hierarchies is to be inclusive and to give a place for all the angels. Thomas Aquinas grasps the nettle and states that Michael is an archangel and therefore belongs to the second lowest order of angels. This shows the tension between the grand cosmic schemes of heavenly hierarchies and devotion to particular angels. What makes Michael an enduring figure is not his place in the hierarchy. In the Jewish tradition Michael is significant because of his role as protector of Israel. In Christianity he is invoked primarily because of his action in fighting against the Devil. It is this fight that is the subject of our next chapter.

7

Fallen Angels

A War in Heaven

Now war arose in heaven, Michael and his angels fighting against the dragon; and the dragon and his angels fought, but they were defeated and there was no longer any place for them in heaven. And the great dragon was thrown down, that ancient serpent, who is called the Devil and Satan, the deceiver of the whole world—he was thrown down to the earth, and his angels were thrown down with him. And I heard a loud voice in heaven, saying, 'Now...the accuser of our brethren has been thrown down, who accuses them day and night before our God...Rejoice then, O heaven and you that dwell there! But woe to you, O earth and sea, for the Devil has come down to you in great wrath, because he knows that his time is short!'   (Revelation 12: 7–12)

This passage is from the book of Revelation, the last book in the New Testament. It paints a vivid picture of spiritual warfare between two forces, the forces of light and the forces of darkness. The forces of light are the angels, but who are the forces of darkness? And where did they come from? The answer from this passage seems to be that the forces of darkness, led by the Devil, who is also called 'the Satan', were originally good angels, but they rebelled and turned against God. The Archangel Michael, as military commander of the angelic army, drives the bad angels from heaven. This is good news for heaven but bad news for the earth, as the bad angels now prowl the earth trying to cause trouble for human beings. Nevertheless, the author of the book of Revelation does not intend any equivalence between the Creator and the Devil. For Judaism, Christianity, and Islam there is only one Creator, and the angels are creatures. If the Devil and his army are fallen angels, then the Devil also is a creature. This is shown by the fact that the Devil directly fights (and loses) against the Archangel Michael. There is no direct fight between God and the Devil.

These 'fallen angels' are also called evil spirits, unclean spirits, or more simply demons. In the Greek world the word 'daimon' was a positive word referring to supernatural creatures midway between gods and human beings. A daimon was someone's spirit, genius, or inspiration. Aristotle called the state of perfect human happiness 'eudaimonia'— having a good daimon. This word is not far from the meaning of angel. However, the word 'daimon' took on a very different and much darker meaning for Jews. This was coloured by a clash between Judaism and Hellenistic (Greek) culture.

The background to this culture clash was the success of Alexander the Great (356–323 BCE) in creating an empire stretching from Egypt to India. The Seleucid Empire lasted 300 years, and its influence lasted many centuries longer, in some ways to the present day. It caused Hellenistic ideas and the Greek language to spread throughout the ancient world. However, the relationship between Judaism and Hellenistic culture was not always happy. In 175 BCE Judea was under the control of the Seleucid king Antiochus Epiphanes (c.215–164 BCE). He decided to enforce Hellenistic culture and to forbid the Jewish religion. This resulted in a vicious persecution, which was followed by a Jewish rebellion led by Judas Maccabeus (c.190–160 BCE). These events are the topic of the books of Maccabees, the first two of which are included in Catholic Bibles. They are sometimes included in Protestant Bibles in the apocrypha.

In the context of the Maccabean revolt the Greek word *daimon* became synonymous with evil spirits and with idolatry. The original positive meaning of the word 'demon' was thus inverted, and this inversion was shaped by the experience of persecution in the name of religion. This is fitting, for just as a demon is an angel that has become vicious, so a persecuting religion is a religion that has become vicious. When religion goes bad, it can go very bad indeed. The demonic is the corruption of something that was once positive, powerful, and holy. Philip Pullman has sought to revive the old positive meaning of daemon. This attempt usefully reminds us that categories of thought can shift and should be subject to criticism. Nevertheless, it is useful to have a word for a malicious spirit, and this is sure to remain the ordinary meaning of the word 'demon'.

Paul the apostle, in one of his letters, encourages Christians to 'Put on the whole armour of God, that you may be able to stand against the wiles of the Devil. For we are not contending against flesh and blood, but against the principalities, against the powers, against the world rulers of this present darkness, against the spiritual hosts of wickedness in the heavenly places' (Ephesians 6: 11–12). Notice that Paul uses the language of warfare: 'armour' and 'contending' against 'principalities' and 'spiritual hosts [armies] of wickedness'. The Devil and his angels are an enemy army and Christians should expect to come under attack.

In the Middle Ages, Christians felt it was very important to be clear that demons had once been good angels and had fallen through their own free will. This was stated authoritatively at a Council of the Church: 'The Devil and the other demons were indeed created by God good by nature but they became bad through themselves; human beings, however, sinned at the suggestion of the Devil' (Creed of Lateran IV). Christians at that time wanted to make clear their belief that the world and everything in it was created by God and that, when it was created, it was 'very good' (Genesis 1: 31). They rejected the idea that there were two gods: a good god and an equally powerful bad god who were constantly struggling against each other. For Christians the Devil is not a bad god but is a good creature that has gone off the rails and turned against his Creator.

How can Angels Sin?

The idea that demons are fallen angels neatly takes care of the question as to what demons are and where they come from. It also avoids holding God responsible for creating such malicious beings. When God created them they were good. They became malicious by their own choice. However, the idea that angels could fall leads to a whole host of other questions. What kind of sin can an angel commit? Human beings are weak creatures with physical needs and desires and limited intelligence or self-control. It is not difficult to see how a human being might be distracted from his or her true good by something immediately appealing. Theft and sexual infidelity are harmful to others and are unworthy actions of human beings, but such actions are common in every society, because they seem to offer a quick route to pleasure and security. For human beings, the right thing to do is not always easy.

In contrast, an angel has no physical needs. There is no need for material possessions or financial security. They do not get hungry or cold or tired. They are not flesh and blood. Angels do not feel bodily desires. Furthermore, whereas human beings are often ignorant and confused about what is good for them, it seems that angels would have a much clearer vision of what is good for them. But, if angels have clear self-knowledge and live in the presence of God, why would they ever leave that presence? Why would they make a choice that they must see is harmful to them?

Jews and Christians have put forward several suggestions as to the kind of sin that the angels committed, but two are most prominent. The first suggestion is that the sin of the angels was pride. Pride is the kind of failing that occurs not to the weak or the unhappy but to the talented and contented. It is precisely because angels are so clear-minded and so superior to human beings in various ways that angels could become proud. The pride of the angels caused them to appreciate their own greatness more than they appreciated the source of that greatness in their Creator. Thomas Aquinas argued that the pride of the Devil expressed itself as a desire to be like God. Now there is an irony here, because, according to Thomas, the good angels were made to be like God, because they were to receive a share of God's life. If the Devil had accepted the gift of God's life, then he would have become like God. However, the Devil wanted to achieve this end by his own effort. For this reason, Anselm of Canterbury (1033–1109) said that the Devil 'grasped at that end which he would have come to had he remained faithful'.

The other sin that is often attributed to the angels is envy, not envy of God but envy of human beings. As noted above, the Talmud describes the negative reaction of the angels when God states his intention to create Adam. According to the eleventh-century Rabbi Moses ha-Darshan in his Midrash on Genesis, the fall is a direct consequence of the refusal of the Satan to worship Adam. This is very closely parallel to the Quran, where the fall of Iblis is linked to his refusal to acknowledge Adam: 'We told the angels, "Prostrate to Adam", and they prostrated, except Iblis (the Satan)' (7: 11–12; see also 2: 34; 15: 28–31; 20: 116; 38: 71–4).

This raises a further question: when did the angels fall? Was it before the material creation or was it later? If the angels fell as a result of being envious of Adam, then it seems that this happened after the world had begun. According to Thomas Aquinas, angels were faced with a choice at the first moment of their existence—they either acknowledged God whole-heartedly and made this acknowledgement the whole meaning of their existence, or they preferred their own choices independent of their Creator.

There is a difference here between Aquinas and Dante, for Dante described a class of indifferent angels who had made a choice neither in favour of God nor against God. This may be a part of his wish to defend an idea of a secular realm somehow independent of God. In contrast, Aquinas had rejected the idea of indifferent angels. There are good angels and bad angels, but angels do not sit on the fence. When they act, they act with their whole self.

For human beings, to live is to change, but Aquinas thought that angels were not changeable in this way. Angels dwell in eternity with God and do not experience time and emotion as human beings do. So, Aquinas reasoned, if angels fell, they fell right at the beginning and they stay fallen, while, if they chose to be with God, they remain with God.

Djinn are not Fallen Angels

Within Christianity, and in later Judaism, it is clear that demons are not a different kind of being from angels but are simply angels that have gone off the rails. However, there are strands of ancient Judaism that are far less clear about the essential identity of angels and demons. There is a passage in the Talmud that suggests that demons are a third kind of creature, midway between human beings and angels.

The rabbis taught: Six things are said with regard to demons, three in which they are like the angels: they have wings, they float from one end of the world to the other, and they know what is about to be; and three in which they are like men: they eat and drink, they are fruitful and multiply, and they are mortal.

If demons eat, drink, reproduce, and die, then clearly they have bodies of some kind and are not pure spirits. This provides the context for looking at Islamic views of demons.

Within Islam, demons (shaitans) are not angels but are a third kind of being: they are djinn. They are different in kind from angels, for, whereas angels are created from light, djinn are created from 'smokeless fire'. Thus they are slightly more tangible than angels but not heavy like human beings.

In the West, the most famous example of a djinn is the 'genie of the lamp' from the *Book of One Thousand and One Nights*. This is an appropriate place to start thinking about djinn, for they are creatures of Arab folklore. They were the subject of folk tales both before and after the writing of the Quran. In these stories it is clear that djinn are not purely good, like the angels. They can be good or bad, helpful to human beings or harmful. There are some similarities here between djinn and the fairies or nature spirits of other cultures—capricious and powerful beings who should be respected but should not be trusted.

Djinn are mentioned in various places in the Quran but especially in the chapter devoted to them, Sura 72. Here it is made clear that djinn have free will. Some are righteous and submit their wills to God while others are 'less than righteous' (72: 11). Hence, while all demons are djinn, not all djinn are demons. There are good djinn too.

The Satan: Adversary and Tempter

There are many angels (or djinn) who fell and became demons, but there is also one chief demon. In Hebrew he is called the Satan, which means 'the adversary'. Satan is not a proper name in Hebrew, like David or John, it is always a title or description. It is not Satan but always *the* Satan. This word was sometimes translated into Greek by a word that means 'the accuser': *diabolos*. This is the origin for the English word 'devil'. The Quran talks of the Shaitan exactly parallel to the Satan in Hebrew. It also talks of many shaitans in the same way as we would talk of many devils. Interestingly, the name given to the Shaitan in the Quran, Iblis, seems to be derived from Greek word *diabolos*. So a Hebrew word, translated into Greek and then transliterated in Arabic, becomes the Islamic name of the Devil.

Judaism, Christianity, and Islam have much in common in what they say about the Satan. All accept that there is such a creature. All view the Satan as the enemy of the human race. All teach that the Satan was once good and fell through his own free will. None makes the Satan an evil god. For the Abrahamic faiths there is only one God, and God is good. To think that the Satan is equivalent to the personification of all evil is to overstate his importance. The Satan is simply a creature who turned away from his true happiness and now seeks to spoil the happiness of human creatures.

There are close similarities in what Islam and the Judaeo-Christian tradition have to say about the Satan, but there are also some differences. In Judaism and Christianity the Satan is a fallen angel. It is generally believed he was created to be the highest or most powerful angel, sometimes called Lucifer, the morning star (from Isaiah 14: 12). In Islam, Iblis is a djinn. There are some passages in the Quran where he might seem to be an angel (for example, 2: 34), but these in fact only show him with the angels. In other passages he is described as made from fire (7: 12) as djinn are, and in one passage he is described as 'of the djinn' (18: 50). Why is it that in Islam there is resistance to seeing the Satan or the other demons as fallen angels? It is because such a fall can happen only through the use of free will, and, according to Islam, angels have no free will, they are purely and inescapably good. They cannot fall. On this point, the Christian thinker Thomas Aquinas was close to the Islamic view. Aquinas also thought that angels, because they live in eternity and see God, cannot fall or change their minds in a fundamental way. Nevertheless, he thought that angels did have a fundamental choice, once and for all, at the moment they were created, and at this point they could fall, and some of them did.

The Hebrew Bible begins with the story of creation, followed immediately by the story of the fall of Adam and Eve. The first human couple sin because they are tempted by a 'snake' that is 'more subtle than any other wild creature that the Lord God had made' (Genesis 3: 1). In this original version of the story there is no explicit mention of the Satan.

The Satan is first mentioned explicitly some hundreds of years later in the book of Job. In this book the angels (literally 'the sons of God') are with God, and the Satan is with them. God boasts of how faithful Job is, and the Satan asks to be allowed to test Job's faith. The Satan is the tempter who tries to make Job curse God. The beginning of the Job story is very like the Islamic (and Talmudic) story of the Satan among the angels refusing to bow down to Adam. It shows the Satan as a tempter whose role is to test human beings. Still at this point there is no identification of the Satan with the snake in the story of Adam and Eve.

In later Judaism and in Christianity the snake is identified explicitly with the Satan. The New Testament refers to 'that ancient serpent, who is called the Devil and Satan' (Revelation 12: 9). The snake is the Devil. In the Quran it is the Satan who whispers to human beings: 'Your Lord did not forbid you [to eat] from this tree, except to prevent you from becoming angels, and from attaining eternal existence' (7: 20). There is no mention of any snake.

In the Islamic story it is not clear how the Satan can get into paradise to tempt Adam, as he has already been expelled from there. Some scholars argue that Adam and Eve were near the edge of the garden and the Satan whispered from outside. There is a folk tale that the Satan came back disguised as a speck of dust between the teeth of the snake. This story has no weight in Islam, but it makes the connection between the Satan and the snake. The snake symbolizes what is twisted and dangerous. Evil hides itself like a snake in the grass.

In all three Abrahamic traditions the primary activity of the Satan is to tempt human beings to do what is evil. As the enemy of the human race the Satan aims not to harm human beings directly but to get human beings to harm themselves. This is well expressed by the Islamic description of the Satan as the whisperer. The Satan whispers into the human heart, but it is still human beings who have freedom and responsibility who act. Human beings can either follow these whispers and do the wrong thing, or ignore these whispers and do the right thing. The same theme is explored in the satirical Christian classic *The Screwtape Letters*. In these letters a senior devil instructs his nephew on how to tempt human beings.

In popular culture, in films and cartoons, it is common to represent the inner struggle of conscience and temptation as an argument between a devil (on the left shoulder) and a guardian angel (on the right shoulder). This idea has an echo in the Jewish story from the Talmud that on the way back from the synagogue a man is accompanied by two angels, a good angel and an evil angel. The image of the 'shoulder angel' can be traced back to the Quran, where it states that each person has two recording angels, keeping a tally of their deeds (50: 17). The idea that these recording angels were on the shoulder was perhaps influenced by the saying of the prophet that you should not spit over your right shoulder—because there is an angel there—but you may spit over your left shoulder.

According to Judaism, Christianity, and Islam, human temptation began with the Satan in paradise, and it is common to represent all temptation as coming from the Devil (or from individual devils). However, even those who believe in the existence of demonic tempters who whisper in the human heart need not believe that every temptation is from a demon. Thomas Aquinas said that human beings were quite capable of being tempted by attractive or by fearful things, without having to be prodded by a devil. To imagine that everything that goes wrong in the world and every sin is the immediate work of the Satan is to overstate his power and influence. All good things come from God. But the Satan is not responsible for all the bad in the world. The Satan is simply a spoilsport who wishes to cause as much trouble as he can for the human race. Like every creature, his power is limited.

Magic and the Invocation of Demons

While the power of angels and demons is limited, it is still in some ways superior to the power of human beings. Angels are 'above' human beings. Thinkers such as Thomas Aquinas argued that the intellectual powers of angels were far in advance of anything even the greatest human mind is capable of. In particular, angels have some knowledge of the future. It is no surprise, then, that throughout history some people have tried to tap into this angelic knowledge.

According to the Quran (2: 102), black magic had its origin with two angels, Harut and Marut. These angels taught sorcery to the Babylonians, and this has since been used by demons. This black magic can be used to separate a man from his wife and to do other kinds of harm. However, though this sorcery has been harmful and used by demons, the angels Harut and Marut were not themselves evil. They tempted people because this was what they were sent to do, but they did not desire that people should disobey God. In contrast, the demons used this magic to encourage people to do evil.

Those who attempt to gain power or knowledge from angels often appeal to good angels. For example, the seventeenth century occultist John Dee (1527–1608) carved a 'holy table', which he used to communicate with angels and with souls of the dead. Through a medium called Edward Kelly (1555–97), he allegedly conjured up and conversed with the Archangel Uriel. It was Uriel who instructed him of the characters that are written on the table, representing the language of angels. This was not, in Dee's mind, an attempt to use demons.

Nevertheless, it does reduce angels to a source of power. The difference between this attitude and a religious attitude is well summed up by the philosopher Wittgenstein: 'Religious faith and superstition are quite different. One of them results from *fear* and is a sort of false science. The other is a trusting.'

The eccentric activities of John Dee were a kind of false science, but they were not explicitly Satanic. Far worse were the alleged activities of Gilles de Rais (1404–40), a nobleman and one time companion of Joan of Arc who practised child murder in the search for occult power. While Joan was herself accused of witchcraft, her motivation was an expression of her Catholic faith. In the sharpest contrast, it seems that Gilles de Rais was willing to do whatever was necessary, even commit unspeakable crimes, for the sake of wielding supernatural power.

Satanism and Romantic Rebellion

If the social order is itself harmful, then rebelling against that order can be a positive or a virtuous thing. From the Protestant Reformation to the American War of Independence, there have been examples of human rebellion that are widely admired. Even those who remain faithful to an old order can admire the nobility of spirit of those who rebel. The courage to resist a perceived wrong is a profoundly human thing.

Nevertheless, there can be a romantic idealization of rebellion, even where there is no real reason to rebel. The 'rebel without a cause' is a romantic figure because he (typically he) fights against everything without a sense of a better alternative. This attraction to rebellion without a positive direction lies at the root of Satanism and those subcultures that use death, evil, and the Devil as badges of membership. These movements flourish at times when the accepted moral order is thought of as both restrictive and hypocritical. Rebellion is then experienced as a kind of liberation and a form of honesty—the honesty of shamelessness and blasphemy. Examples could be found from Gilles de Rais to the comparatively innocent self-indulgence of hellfire clubs of the eighteenth century (where dissolute aristocrats sought out deliberately blasphemous pleasures) to the deliberate sexual perversions of the Marquis de Sade (1740–1814). By the nineteenth century there were organized Satanist cults. This is vividly described by the novelist Joris-Karl Huysmans (1848–1907).

While there are still Satanic cults, the dominant expression of self-destructive rebellion in contemporary culture is in heavy metal music, as evident from names such as Black Sabbath and Judas Priest. It is perhaps also evident in the Hells Angels Motorcycle Club. In these examples there is a question about whether this rebellion is a symbolic safety valve—a form of catharsis—or whether it is harmful and self–destructive. In favour of the more benign interpretation would be the example of a character such as Ozzy Osbourne (1948–) who founded Black Sabbath and was accused of complicity in the suicide of two teenagers, but who by 2002 had become such an establishment figure that he was invited to a White House dinner. There is all the difference in the world between the adolescent shock value of blasphemous music and the truly demonic Gilles de Rais. Nevertheless, these contemporary subcultures of romantic rebellion cannot be

Figure 15 Hells Angels take their name from rebel or fallen *angels*.

regarded as altogether innocent or healthy. They commonly foster excessive risk-taking, substance abuse, criminality, suicide, and other forms of self-harm.

Sexual Relations with Demons

When men began to multiply on the face of the ground, and daughters were born to them, the sons of God saw that the daughters of men were fair; and they took to wife such of them as they chose ... The Nephilim were on the earth in those days, and also afterward, when the sons of God came in to the daughters of men, and they bore children to them. These were the mighty men that were of old, the men of renown. (Genesis 6: 1, 2, 4)

125

This short paragraph from the book of Genesis is possibly the strangest passage in the entire Hebrew Bible. It seems to suggest that the angels fell because they were attracted by female beauty, and that after the angels had fallen they married women and their children were giants (which is how *nephilim* is sometimes translated). There is an interesting echo of this story in the film *City of Angels*. Nevertheless, it goes strongly against most of what we have said thus far about angels. If angels do not have bodies, then why would they feel the attractions of physical beauty? And, more importantly, how could they father children?

This story of intercourse between angels and women is repeated and indeed expanded in some Jewish books such as Enoch and Jubilees. These books were written around the time of Jesus—later than the Hebrew Bible but before the Talmud. In these versions of the story, the angels who fell are named as Azazel and Samhazai. Both marry and have children. Later Samhazai repents and he returns to a place halfway between earth and heaven, but Azazel remains on earth and is mentioned in the Bible as a demon who dwells in the desert (Leviticus 16: 10; see the Revised Standard Version; other versions translate Azazel as 'scapegoat').

The later Jewish tradition gives a different interpretation of this biblical passage, according to which 'sons of God' did not refer to angels but to those who held high office among the people. Christian writers such as Augustine interpreted the sons of God as descendants of Seth, and daughters of men as descendants of Cain. Under either interpretation, the story is not literally about angels but about privileged groups of human beings.

Nevertheless, even while Augustine states that this passage does not refer to angels, he does think that demons can and do have intercourse with women—these are the gods of the woods: fauns or satyrs 'which common people call incubi'. Augustine alleges that many reliable people have experienced these things. It seems that people used the concept of the incubus to describe unwanted and disturbing erotic dreams. It is this experience that they attributed to demons. Certainly Augustine does not mention any evidence that children were born as a result of a visit by an incubus.

There is a temptation in the popular imagination to think that a child could literally be the child of the Devil. In the film *Rosemary's Baby* this theme is used to explore the common anxieties of pregnancy, the feeling that a woman's body is somehow being taken over. In *The Omen* the same theme takes on the dimension of global conspiracy and fears about the end of the world (beautifully satirized in *Good Omens* by Terry Pratchett and Neil Gaimon).

In the past the idea of a devil-child was sometimes used to express and to excuse the rejection of a child with disability or behavioural disorder. Such a child was not the true offspring of the parents. He or she was a 'changeling'. Thomas Aquinas, however, was very clear that no angel or demon could ever produce a child. Procreation is a natural biological power that angels and demons do not possess. The only possibility Aquinas allows is if a demon assumed the form of a woman (succubus) and had intercourse with a man and then transformed itself into the form of a man (incubus) and impregnated the woman with the man's seed. In this way a child could be conceived, but, Thomas wrote triumphantly, it would not be the child of the demon but the child of the man! There are no demon-children, only troubled children who have been demonized.

Possession by Demons

And immediately there was in their synagogue a man with an unclean spirit; and he cried out, 'What have you to do with us, Jesus of Nazareth? Have you come to destroy us? I know who you are, the Holy One of God.' But Jesus rebuked him, saying, 'Be silent, and come out of him!' And the unclean spirit, convulsing him and crying with a loud voice, came out of him. And they were all amazed, so that they questioned among themselves, saying, 'What is this? A new teaching! With authority he commands even the unclean spirits, and they obey him.'   (Mark 1: 23–7)

The New Testament contains many stories of Jesus casting out demons. Typically, the demon will recognize Jesus and speak to him. Jesus will forbid the demon to speak and will then command it to leave the person. As it leaves, the demon may cause the person to fall down or cry out, but after it has gone the person is 'in his right mind' (Mark 5: 15).

In one famous story a man has many demons. Jesus asks, 'What is your name?' and the man replies, 'My name is Legion; for we are many' (Mark 5: 9). The demons then beg Jesus, who is about to cast them out, to allow them to enter a herd of pigs. He allows this, 'and the herd, numbering about two thousand, rushed down the steep bank into the sea, and were drowned in the sea' (Mark 5: 13). It is not clear what advantage the demons get from this, but the effect on the pigs shows the power that was oppressing the man. Pigs are regarded as unclean animals in Judaism, and by association show that demons are also unclean. In the Gospel of Mark demons are frequently referred to as 'unclean spirits'.

When Jesus casts out demons, he does it by his own authority. He does not invoke the Archangel Michael, or Abraham, or Solomon, or anyone else. It is by his own authority, because of who he is, that he commands demons. This leads some critics to accuse Jesus of being in league with the Devil. 'He is possessed by Be-elzebul, and by the prince of demons he casts out the demons' (Mark 3: 22). Jesus replies with a question: 'How can Satan cast out Satan?' (Mark 3: 23). It is not in the Satan's interest to reduce his kingdom or to free people from the power of demons. For Jesus, and for the early followers of Jesus, the authority of Jesus over demons was a sign that a new era was dawning and the kingdom of God was being established on earth.

Jesus and his followers were not the only Jewish exorcists working at that time. Josephus tells of a man called Eleazar who invoked the name of Solomon to expel demons. He took a root mentioned by Solomon and inserted it into a ring. Then he put this ring in the possessed man's nostrils and drew the demon out through the nostrils. A rabbinic writer from this period gave the advice that, if an evil spirit had entered someone, then to make the demon flee you should burn the roots of herbs under him and surround him with water. The burning of roots to drive away the Devil echoes the book of Tobit, where Raphael burns the heart and liver of a fish to drive out the demon Asmodeus (Tobit 6: 17). The idea of exorcism is thus contained within Judaism, but it has been much more prominent in some traditions than others. It is associated in particular with German and middle European Judaism in the Middle Ages and the Early Modern period, with the Cabala, and with Hasidic Judaism.

The concepts of possession and of exorcism of evil djinn are also found in Islam. One verse in the Quran compares those who charge interest on a loan to those 'controlled by the Satan' (2: 275). More significantly, there is a story of the prophet Muhammad performing an exorcism. He opens the afflicted boy's mouth and blows into it three times, saying: 'In the name of Allah, I am the slave of Allah, get out, enemy of Allah!'

It should be noticed that this story does not carry the weight of the Quran, and the passage in the Quran is open to different interpretations. Hence there are some Muslims scholars who do not think that possession by djinn really occurs. Nevertheless, it is a matter of Islamic belief that djinn exist, and the practice of casting out evil djinn has been maintained by Muslims up to the present day.

The idea of demon possession is present to a greater or lesser extent within Christianity, Judaism, and Islam. Nevertheless, in all three there is a caution about attributing symptoms to demons or to djinn for physical or psychiatric disorders. For example, in the New Testament a child is said to have a demon that 'seizes him, it dashes him down; and he foams and grinds his teeth and becomes rigid' (Mark 9: 18). This certainly sounds very like epilepsy. Other symptoms sound like dissociative identity disorder, schizophrenia, or Tourette's syndrome. Whatever may be said about ancient stories, when faced with a contemporary case it is important to identify the cause of the affliction, whether physical, psychiatric, or supernatural. Hence the Roman Catholic Church, which continues to practice exorcism, requires that physical or mental causes be ruled out before authorization of the rite of exorcism. A similar caution is found among contemporary rabbinic and Islamic scholars. Nevertheless, it must be admitted that in all three faiths there are more popular forms of religion that are less discriminating about when to perform an exorcism. If an enthusiasm for casting out demons prevents adequate physical or psychiatric care, then it could actually harm the person.

The idea of exorcism often fascinates people who are not themselves religious, and films such as *The Exorcist* (1973) or, more recently, *The Exorcism of Emily Rose* (2005), continue to arouse interest, particularly as both are loosely based on historical cases. For those who are religious, there is often ambivalence about this subject. If interest in angels is not the centre of religion, interest in demons is still less central. Even if there are some individuals who are directly afflicted by demons, the more significant role of demons is to tempt or inspire human beings to harm themselves and others. Human wickedness is the result of human choices, the result of free decisions in which the Satan is really no more than an agent provocateur.

8

Wrestling with Angels

Jacob and the Angel

And Jacob was left alone; and a man wrestled with him until the breaking of the day. When the man saw that he did not prevail against Jacob, he touched the hollow of his thigh; and Jacob's thigh was put out of joint as he wrestled with him. Then he said, 'Let me go, for the day is breaking.' But Jacob said, 'I will not let you go, unless you bless me.'

And he said to him, 'What is your name?' And he said, 'Jacob.'

Then he said, 'Your name shall no more be called Jacob, but Israel, for you have striven with God and with men, and have prevailed.'

Then Jacob asked him, 'Tell me, I pray, your name.' But he said, 'Why is it that you ask my name?' And there he blessed him.

So Jacob called the name of the place Peniel, saying, 'For I have seen God face to face, and yet my life is preserved.'   (Genesis 32: 24–30)

The angel in this story does not come as a messenger, like Gabriel, or as a healer, like Raphael. The angel does not come to test Jacob's hospitality, as do the three angels who visit Abraham. This angel comes in the darkness of the night to contend with Jacob, to test his spirit and his resolve. Jacob prevails and lives to see the sun rise, though we are told that later he survives limping (Genesis 32: 25). The whole encounter is somewhat mysterious. Jacob meets God and is blessed by God, but before he is blessed he has to grapple with God. The angel is not an evil spirit, but is a formidable spirit.

This scene was rarely portrayed before the nineteenth century. Rembrandt (1606–69) is an exception. However, the imagery has a great resonance in the modern world. Just as Paul Klee struggles to see angels that are other than 'incomplete', 'forgetful', and 'still ugly', so a variety of nineteenth- and twentieth-century artists were inspired by this struggle between man and angel. Eugène Delacroix (1798–1863), Gustave Moreau (1826–98), Paul Gauguin (1848–1903), Odilon Redon (1840–1916), Jacob Epstein (1880–1959), and Marc Chagall (1887–1985) all produced memorable images of this encounter. In the case of Gauguin, the painting is called *Vision after a Sermon*. The picture features a group of women in Breton costume talking and praying. The figures of Jacob and the angel, pictured against a vivid red background, are not naturalistic, but the contest has more earthy vitality than it has the stillness of an icon. It occurs in their imagination, but is nonetheless real for that.

The title 'wrestling with angels' has been adopted for several modern collections of poems and short stories, and for works as diverse as: a history of Jews in Los Angeles; a study of Jewish attitudes to the use of military power by Israel; a reflection on surviving cancer; a discussion of sexuality and the Church; and many more besides. It provides the title of a biography of the New Zealand novelist Janet Frame (1924–2004) and also of the biographical film of Jewish playwright and gay-rights activist Tony Kushner (1956–), which features, among other things, Emma Thompson

Figure 16 *Gauguin painted a group of women remembering a sermon of Jacob wrestling with the angel.*

as an angel who crashes through a ceiling. *Wrestling with Angels* is also the title of a book by Rowan Williams, the Archbishop of Canterbury. It is subtitled *Conversations in Modern Theology.*

These works of art and literature depict a spiritual struggle that is characteristically modern. The image of grappling with the angel expresses a common experience. The religious meaning of the past is not denied, but this meaning is elusive and comes only with difficulty. Jacob wins the day and receives his blessing, but he enters into life limping.

Holding up a Mirror to Humanity

A running theme in this book has been that reflection on angels can illuminate aspects of human existence. In the Abrahamic traditions, serious discussion of angels has often been a roundabout way of talking about human beings: angelology as disguised anthropology.

Angels frequently highlight moments of human significance. Angels are present at sacred moments at the beginning and the end of life. Not only the birth of a child but already his or her conception is the beginning of something new. This is revealed by the presence of angels at conception. People rarely reflect that they did not always exist. Yet each person's life is something radically new, something never repeated, something mysterious. It has human meaning from the very beginning.

Angels are also present at the end. Their presence reminds us of the need for spiritual care at the end of life. Thanks to the work of Elisabeth Kübler-Ross (1926–2004) and others, there has been a revival of interest in 'dying well' among psychologists and healthcare workers. The association of angels with dying expresses hope not just for life after death but for meaning in death. This is a great challenge and is a context where people may well speak of wrestling with angels.

In addition to marking the great transitions of beginning and ending, angels also bear witness to the overlooked significance of human life. This is true of overlooked lives, of people who are marginal in terms of social standing or human capacities. Not only does each and every person

Figure 17 Clarence Oddbody, Angel Second Class, is appointed George Bailey's guardian angel in *It's a Wonderful Life.*

have a guardian angel, but the examples of St Martin of Tours and of Dorothy Day show that 'entertaining angels' can help people to recognize the stranger in front of them.

Angels can also call attention to the significance of events within life. This is the theme of the film *It's a Wonderful Life*. The angel, Clarence Oddbody, shows the despairing George Bailey the true effects of his actions. This helps George see the impact of many small and ordinary acts of kindness and the cumulative effect of a good life on those around. More importantly, it reminds him what and who he values in life. His despair had been inward-looking. The angel shows him his connectedness with others and gives him hope.

The significance of human experience is also explored in the beautiful German film *Wings of Desire*. This shows angels in Berlin watching and accompanying the people of that city. The story is of one angel who gets fed up with watching eternally 'from above' and who wants to immerse himself in the river of time—to experience the 'now and now' and to touch and taste and feel the world. The angel acts as a mirror by way of contrast. Human beings are not angels and recognizing this can lead to a new appreciation of the richness of human life.

A Time of Angels

Lynn Townsend White (1907–87), in an influential essay in 1967, accused Christianity (and by implication Judaism and Islam) of bearing 'a huge burden of guilt' for the emerging ecological crisis. The root problem was alleged to be that Christians saw human beings as the peak of creation. Only human beings were made in 'the image of God' (Genesis 1: 27) and are thus given 'dominion' over the rest of creation (Genesis 1: 28). This idea all too easily flowed into an attitude of domination or exploitation. Other living things had value only if they were useful for human beings. This utilitarian attitude towards creation has led to a crisis that is threatening the whole planet with disaster.

While the anthropocentric arrogance detected by White may have its roots in a distortion of Christianity, this problematic attitude is further amplified in some strands of secular thinking. For atheist philosophers such as Ludwig Feuerbach (1804–72) or Bertrand Russell (1872–1970), the existence of God and of spiritual beings 'above' human beings represents a threat to human freedom. Human beings are and ought to be in control of the world. Nature is an object to be controlled. Nothing is sacred. This is seen even in the writings of Philip Pullman, for whom God must be killed and angels overthrown so that heaven is no longer a kingdom but a 'republic of heaven'. Human beings then become the source of all value.

Reflection on the angels can help remedy this. If human beings are 'a little lower than the angels' (Psalm 8: 5, LXX version), then we are midway up a chain of being, not at the top looking down on everyone else. Similarly, the idea of an angelic 'song of the spheres' expresses the beauty and integrity of the whole cosmos. Human beings take their place in this whole and not over and against the rest of creation. This is also seen in the tableau of Raphael, Tobias, and the dog (Tobit 6: 1–2), which is an image of the microcosm, of angelic, human, and other animal life. The tableau shows a shared journey, a spiritual pilgrimage. It is not a journey that is complete nor can it be completely understood before it ends.

Angels have taken different forms in different times and places. They have carried different cultural meanings. Nevertheless there are recurrent patterns. Angels are liminal figures at the threshold between the visible and the invisible worlds. The stories of angels are often playful or ironic. In the words of Chesterton, 'angels can fly because they can take themselves lightly'.

Images and ideas about angels have moved easily between different religions and into contemporary culture. This is another reason why Judaism, Islam, and Christianity have sometimes been ambivalent about them. Angels do not stay safely in the confines of any one religion. Talk of angels has always flourished more in folk culture than in official categories. They help illuminate the limitedness of those categories and teach us to be suspicious of easy rationalism, whether of a secular or of a religious kind. The world is not tidy, and it is neither fruitful nor honest to tidy it up artificially. Angels help show up the mystery of it all.

The elusive character of angels helps explain why they remain popular in an age that finds faith difficult. This is why Iris Murdoch described this age as a 'time of angels' and even wrote that, if there is no God, the angels are set free. Yet, if the angels have been 'set free' in our modern irreligious culture, as their popularity seems to attest, then nevertheless, like homing pigeons, they should be allowed to circle and return to their source. One aim of this book has been to encourage people to see angels in their original habitat. This is not in an attempt to constrain the significance that people find in angels. It is rather an invitation to add to this and to trace the meaning of angels back to the spiritual tradition that begins with Abraham, whether through its Jewish, Christian, or Islamic forms.

Until the end of the book I have avoided, as far as possible, asking directly about the evidence for angels. So what do I think? Do angels really exist? It seems to me foolish to seek to prove the existence of angels. It would be like deliberately testing a friendship—something likely to do more harm than good. The desire to test everything stems from a preference for knowledge over trust. Yet we cannot live unless we sometimes trust. On the other hand, if attempting to prove the existence of angels is folly, attempting to exclude the possibility of angels a priori seems to me a greater folly. Denying the possibility of angels can be done only by reducing all reality to physical categories, to matter in motion. Yet human beings possess an inner life, are aware, come to understand, act freely, make moral judgements, commit themselves to one another and to greater causes. This cannot all be expressed in purely physical or quantitative terms. For the sake of humanity, then, it is necessary to defend the human spirit, and this implies keeping an open mind about the existence of other, immaterial, spirits.

The contemporary preoccupation with angels is an embarrassment to many religious believers and an affront to many atheists. Yet this is a time of the angels. The visitors who once sat at Abraham's table are still here. They show no sign of taking flight from modern culture. They prefer to remain, whether to inspire us, to console us, or to wrestle against us.

FURTHER READING

ORIGINAL SOURCES

A good place to start with further reading is with the original sources for stories and speculation about angels. This introduction has included many references to the Jewish Scriptures, the New Testament, and the Quran, so that the reader can follow these up. It is also worth searching the Bible or the Quran, as there are several easily available web-based versions. Two are worth mentioning: the Blue Letter Bible (www. blueletterbible.org) and the Quran Search at IslamiCity (www. islamicity.com/QuranSearch). These are helpful, because they include the original languages and more than one English translation.

There is no searchable version of the Talmud, but there are many references to the Talmud in the excellent article by Ludwig Blau and Kaufman Kohler, 'Angelology', in Cyrus Adler (ed.), *The Jewish Encyclopedia* (New York: Funk and Wagnalls, 1906–10), www.jewishencyclopedia.com/ view.jsp?letter=A&artid=1521.

It is then possible to look up the references in a web-based version of the Talmud at www.come-and-hear.com/talmud.

In the References, preference has been given to versions of texts that are available online. However, the newest and most critical editions are not in the public domain. For further reading, see:

James Charlesworth (ed.), *The Old Testament Pseudepigrapha*, vol. i. *Apocalyptic Literature and Testaments* (New Haven: Yale University Press 1983).

—— *The Old Testament Pseudepigrapha*, vol. ii. *Expansions of the 'Old Testament' and Legends, Wisdom and Philosophical Literature, Prayers, Psalms and Odes, Fragments of lost Judeo-Christian Works* (New Haven: Yale University Press 1985).

Dionysius, *Pseudo Dionysius: The Complete Works*, trans. Paul Rorem (Classics of Western Spirituality; New York: Paulist Press, 1988).

Thomas Aquinas, *Summa Theologiae*, vol. ix. *Angels: 1a. 50–64*, trans. Kenelm Foster (Cambridge: Cambridge University Press, 2005).

—— *Summa Theologiae*, vol. xv. *The World Order: 1a. 110–119*, trans. M. J. Charlesworth (Cambridge: Cambridge University Press, 2005).

Steven Chase (ed.), *Angelic Spirituality: Medieval Perspectives on the Ways of Angels* (Classics of Western Spirituality) (New York: Paulist Press, 2002).

ANGELS IN ART AND LITERATURE

For academic discussion of angels in art, see:

Charles Dempsey, *Inventing the Renaissance Putto* (Chapel Hill, NC: University of North Carolina Press, 2001).

Glenn Peers, *Subtle Bodies: Representing Angels in Byzantium* (Berkeley, CA, and London: University of California Press, 2001).

Antony Gormley, *Making an Angel* (London: Booth Clibborn, 1998).

Therese Martin, 'The Development of Winged Angels in Early Christian Art', in *Espacio, Tiempo y Forma, Serie VII, Historia del Arte*, 14 (2001), 11–30.

There are also collections of painting of angels with commentary:

Francesco Buranelli and Robin Dietrick, *Between God and Man: Angels in Italian Art* (Jackson, MS: University Press of Mississippi, 2007).

Rosa Geogr, *Angels and Demons in Art*, trans. Rosanna Giammanco Frongia (Oxford: Oxford University Press, 2005).

James Underhill, *Angels* (Shaftesbury and Rockport, MA: Element, 1995).

The collection by Peter Lamborn Wilson, *Angels* (London: Thames and Hudson, 1980), deliberately includes angel-like beings from other traditions.

General surveys of religious art will also include discussion of angels. For example, John Dillenberger, *A Theology of Artistic Sensibilities: The Visual Arts and the Church* (London: SCM Press, 1987).

For more on angels in literature, see:

David Jeffrey, *A Dictionary of Biblical Tradition in English Literature* (Grand Rapids, MI: Wm B. Eerdmans Publishing Company, 1993).

Robert West, 'Angels', in William B Hunter, Jr. (gen. ed.), *A Milton Encyclopedia* (London: Associated University Press, 1978), 48–51.

—— *Milton and the Angels* (Athens, GA: University of Georgia Press, 1955).

ANGELOLOGY

Two very scholarly works on the history of beliefs about angels are:

David Keck, *Angels and Angelology in the Middle Ages* (Oxford: Oxford University Press, 1998).

A. Walsham and P. Marshall, *Angels in the Early Modern World* (Cambridge: Cambridge University Press, 2006).

On the representation of Jesus as an angel, see:

Margaret Barker, The *Great Angel: A Study of Israel's Second God* (Louisville, KY: Westminster John Knox Press, 1992).

Charles Gieschen, *Angelomorphic Christology: Antecedents and Early Evidence* (Leiden, Boston, and Cologne: Brill, 1998).

Peter Carrell, *Jesus and the Angels: Angelology and the Christology of the Apocalypse of John* (Cambridge: Cambridge University Press, 1997).

For those interested in the Christian theology of angels, see:

Karl Rahner, 'Angels', in Karl Rahner (ed.), *Encyclopedia of Theology: The Concise Sacramentum mundi* (London and New York: Continuum International Publishing Group, 1975).

Cornelius Ernst, 'How to See an Angel', in *Multiple Echo: Explorations in Theology* (London: Darton Longman and Todd, 1979).

Peter Williams, *The Case for Angels* (Carlisle: Paternoster, 2002).

There are also a number of more popular Christian works on angels:

Jane Williams, *Angels* (Oxford: Lion Publishing, 2006).

Billy Graham, *Angels: God's Secret Agents* (London: Hodder and Stoughton, 2004).

Martin Israel, *Angels: Messengers of Grace* (London: SPCK, 1995).

Ladislaus Boros, *Angels and Men* (New York: Seabury Press, 1976).

For Muslim and Jewish works on angels, see, for example:

Shaykh Muhammad Hisham Kabbani, *Angels Unveiled: A Sufi Perspective* (Chicago: Kazi Publications,1996).

Ronald H. Isaacs, *Ascending Jacob's Ladder: Jewish Views of Angels, Demons, and Evil Spirits* (Northvale, NJ: Jason Aronson, 1997).

On Satan, see Jeffrey Burton Russell's five-volume history:

The Devil: Perceptions of Evil from Antiquity to Primitive Christianity (Ithaca, NY: Cornell University Press, 1977).

Satan: The Early Christian Tradition (Ithaca, NY: Cornell University Press, 1981).

Lucifer: The Devil in the Middle Ages (Ithaca, NY: Cornell University Press, 1984).

Mephistopheles: The Devil in the Modern World (Ithaca, NY: Cornell University Press, 1986).

The Prince of Darkness: Radical Evil and the Power of Good in History (Ithaca, NY: Cornell University Press, 1988).

And for those interested in exorcism:

Malachi Martin, *Hostage to the Devil: The Possession and Exorcism of Five Living Americans* (San Francisco: Harper San Francisco, 1992).

IMPLICATIONS

This book grew from an inaugural lecture, David Albert Jones, 'Angels as a Guide to Ethics', *Pastoral Review*, 4/1 (Jan.–Feb. 2008), 11–16.

Mortimer Adler also argues that the idea of angels is helpful in philosophy if we are to avoid angelic fallacies; see *The Angels and Us* (New York: Macmillan Publishing, 1982).

In a slightly different vein, John Cornwell uses the guardian angel as a literary device to offer a gentle critique of Dawkins: *Darwin's Angel: An Angelic Riposte to 'The God Delusion'* (London: Profile Books Ltd, 2008).

REFERENCES

1. A BRIEF HISTORY OF ANGELS

Dante Alighieri, *The Comedy of Dante Alighieri*, trans. Dorothy L. Sayers and Barbara Reynolds (3 vols.; Harmondsworth: Penguin Classics, 1949–62).

Dionysius, *Celestial Hierarchy*, in *Esoterica*, vol. ii. *148–202* (2000), www.esoteric.msu.edu/VolumeII/CelestialHierarchy.html

The Book of Enoch, trans. R. H. Charles (London: SPCK, 1917), www.sacred-texts.com/bib/boe/index.htm

Josephus, *Jewish Wars*, in *The Works of Josephus, Complete and Unabridged New Updated Edition*, trans. William Whiston, AM (Peabody, MA: Hendrickson Publishers, 1987), www.ccel.org/j/josephus/works/josephus.htm

Daniel Chana Matt (ed.), *The Zohar: Book of Enlightenment* (Classics of Western Spirituality; New York: Paulist Press, 1988).

Philip Pullman, *Northern Lights* (London: Scholastic, 1995).

Thomas Aquinas, *Summa Theologica*, trans. Fathers of the English Dominican (New York: Benziger Bros., 1947), www.newadvent.org/summa

Doreen Virtue, *Angel Therapy: Healing Messages for Every Area of your Life.* (Carlsbad, CA: Hay House, 1997).

2. PICTURING ANGELS

Michele Le Doeuff, *The Sex of Knowing*, trans. Kathryn Hamer and Lorraine Code (New York: Routledge, 2003).

Henry Mayr-Harting, *Perceptions of Angels in History: An Inaugural Lecture* (Oxford: Clarendon Press, 1998).

Rainer Maria Rilke, *Duino Elegies*, in *The Selected Poetry of Rainer Maria Rilke*, trans. Stephen Mitchell (New York: Vintage, 1989).

Teresa of Avila, *The Life of St Teresa of Jesus, of the Order of Our Lady of Carmel. Written by Herself*, trans. David Lewis (London: Thomas Baker; New York: Benziger Bros, 1904), www.gutenberg.org/ebooks/8120

Tertullian, *Apology*, in Allan Menzies (ed.), *Ante-Nicene Fathers*, vol. iii. *Latin Christianity: Its Founder, Tertullian* (Edinburgh: T&T Clark; Grand Rapids, MI: Eerdmans Publishing Company, 1885), www.ccel.org/ccel/schaff/anf03.html

3. WHAT IS AN ANGEL?

Aristotle, *Aristotle's Metaphysics*, trans. W. D. Ross (2 vols.; Oxford: Clarendon Press, 1924; rev. 1958), http://classics.mit.edu/Aristotle/metaphysics.html

Plato, 'Phaedo', in *Euthyphro, Apology, Crito, and Phaedo*, trans. Benjamin Jowett (Amherst, NY: Prometheus Books, 1988), http://classics.mit.edu/Plato/phaedo.html

Moses Maimonides, *The Guide for the Perplexed*, trans. Michael Friedländer (New York: Hebrew Publishing Company, 1881), http://books.google.co.uk/books?id=e4GgHMPDok0C

Philip Schaff (ed.), *St. Augustin's: City of God and Christian Doctrine* (Nicene and Post-Nicene Fathers First Series Volume 2; Edinburgh: T&T Clark; Michigan: Eerdmans Publishing Company, 1887), www.ccel.org/ccel/schaff/npnf102.html

Thomas Aquinas, *Summa Theologica*, trans. Fathers of the English Dominican (New York: Benziger Bros, 1947), www.newadvent.org/summa

4. DIVINE MESSENGERS

Emma Heathcote-James, *Seeing Angels* (London: John Blake Publishing, 2002).

Philip Schaff (ed.), *St Augustin's: City of God and Christian Doctrine* (Nicene and Post-Nicene Fathers First Series Volume 2; Edinburgh: T&T Clark; Michigan: Eerdmans Publishing Company, 1887), www.ccel.org/ccel/schaff/npnf102.html

5. MINISTERING SPIRITS

The Arabian Nights: Tales from a Thousand and One Nights, trans. Richard Burton (New York: Random House Inc., 2001).

David Albert Jones, *The Soul of the Embryo: An Enquiry into the Status of the Human Embryo in the Christian Tradition* (London: Continuum, 2004).

Simon Tugwell, *Human Immortality and the Redemption of Death* (London: Darton, Longman and Todd, 1990).

John Henry Newman, *The Dream of Gerontius* (Oxford: Family Publications, 2001), www.newmanreader.org/works/verses/gerontius.html

Sulpitius Severus, *On The Life of St Martin*, trans. Alexander Roberts, in Philip Schaff and Henry Wace (eds.), *Sulpitius Severus, Vincent of Lerins, John Cassian* (Nicene and Post-Nicene Fathers Second Series Volume 11; Edinburgh: T&T Clark; Michigan: Eerdmans Publishing Company, 1894), www.ccel.org/ccel/schaff/npnf211.html

Salley Vickers, *Miss Garnet's Angel* (London and New York: Harper Perennial, 2006).

6. HEAVENLY HOSTS

Bryan Appleyard, *Aliens: Why They Are Here* (London: Scribner, 2005).

Thomas Carlyle, *Sartor Resartus* (World Classics; Oxford: Oxford University Press, 1999).

Dionysius, *Celestial Hierarchy*, in *Esoterica*, vol. ii. *148–202* (2000), www.esoteric.msu.edu/VolumeII/CelestialHierarchy.html

Isaac D'Israeli, *Curiosities of Literature: Consisting of Anecdotes, Characters, Sketches, and Observations, Literary, Critical, and Historical* (Printed for J. Murray, 1791; original from Oxford University), books.google.co.uk/books?id=rVkUAAAAQAAJ

John Dryden, *The Hind and the Panther*, in Paul Hammond and David Hopkins (eds.), *Dryden: Selected Poems* (Annotated English Poets; London: Longman, 2007).

The Book of Enoch, trans. R. H. Charles (London: SPCK, 1917), www.sacred-texts.com/bib/boe/index.htm

Walter Hilton, *The Scale of Perfection*, trans. John Clark and Rosemary Dorward (Classics of Western Spirituality; New York: Paulist Press, 1990).

Rudolf Otto, *The Idea of the Holy*, trans. John Harvey (New York: Oxford University Press, 1968).

Pascal, *Pensées*, trans. A. Krailsheimer (London: Penguin Classics, 2003).

Philo, *On Dreams, That They Are God-Sent*, in *The Works of Philo: Complete and Unabridged*, New Updated Edition, trans. Charles Duke Yonge (Peabody, MA: Hendrickson Publishers, 1993), www.earlychristianwritings.com/yonge/book21.html (this is a convenient place to find Philo's works, but it should be noted that Philo was a Jew and not an 'early Christian writer').

Rupert Sheldrake and Matthew Fox, *The Physics of Angels: Exploring the Realm Where Science and Spirit Meet* (San Francisco: Harper San Francisco, 1996).

Thomas Aquinas, *Summa Theologica*, trans. Fathers of the English Dominican (New York: Benziger Bros., 1947), www.newadvent. org/summa

Eric Von Däniken, *Chariots of the Gods: Was God An Astronaut?* (London: Souvenir Press Ltd, 1990).

7. FALLEN ANGELS

Clive Staples Lewis, *The Screwtape Letters: Letters from a Senior to a Junior Devil* (Fount edn.; London: HarperCollins, 1998).

Joris-Karl Huysmans, *The Damned (Là-Bas)*, trans. Terry Hale (London: Penguin Classics, 2002).

Philip Schaff (ed.), *St. Augustin's: City of God and Christian Doctrine* (Nicene and Post-Nicene Fathers First Series Volume 2; Edinburgh: T&T Clark; Michigan: Eerdmans Publishing Company, 1887), www.ccel.org/ccel/schaff/npnf102.html

Thomas Aquinas, *Summa Theologica*, trans. Fathers of the English Dominican (New York: Benziger Bros., 1947), www.newadvent. org/summa

Josephus, *Antiquities of the Jews*, in *The Works of Josephus, Complete and Unabridged New Updated Edition*, trans. William Whiston, AM (Peabody, MA: Hendrickson Publishers, 1987), www.ccel.org/ccel/josephus/works/files/works.html

8. WRESTLING WITH ANGELS

Doug Beardsley, *Wrestling with Angels: New and Selected Poems 1960–1995* (Montreal and Quebec: Vehicule, 1995).

References

Phil Blazer and Sherry Portnoy, *Wrestling with the Angels: A History of Jewish Los Angeles* (Encino, CA: Blazer Communications, 2006).

G. K. Chesterton, *Orthodoxy* (San Francisco: Ignatius, 1995).

John J. Clayton, *Wrestling with Angels: New and Collected Stories* (New Milford, CT: Toby Press, 2007).

Marjorie Coppock, *Wrestling with Angels: The Sexual Revolution Confronts the Church* (Eugene, OR: ACW Press, 2003).

Jean-Paul Kauffmann, *The Struggle with the Angel: Delacroix, Jacob, and the God of Good and Evil* (New York: Four Walls Eight Windows, 2002).

Michael King, *Wrestling with the Angel: A Life of Janet Frame* (Auckland: Penguin, 2000).

Elisabeth Kübler-Ross, *On Death and Dying* (New York: Scribner 1997).

Ehud Luz, *Wrestling with an Angel: Power, Morality, and Jewish Identity*, trans. Michael Swirsky (New Haven: Yale University Press, 2003).

Iris Murdoch, *The Time of the Angels* (London: Vintage, 2002).

Philip Pullman, *The Amber Spyglass* (London: Scholastic, 1995).

Rowan Williams and Mike Higton, *Wrestling with Angels: Conversations in Modern Theology* (London: SCM Press, 2007).

INDEX OF LOCORUM

BIBLE

153

QURAN

SUBJECT INDEX

Subject Index